California Bar Examination

Performance Tests and Selected Answers

July 2013

The State Bar Of California
Committee of Bar Examiners/Office of Admissions

180 Howard Street • San Francisco, CA 94105-1639 • (415) 538-2300
845 S. Figueroa Street • Los Angeles, CA 90017-2515 • (213) 765-1500

PERFORMANCE TESTS AND SELECTED ANSWERS

JULY 2013

CALIFORNIA BAR EXAMINATION

This publication contains the two Performance Tests from the July 2013 California Bar Examination and two selected answers for each test.

The answers were assigned high grades and were written by applicants who passed the examination after one read. The answers were produced as submitted by the applicant, except that minor corrections in spelling and punctuation were made for ease in reading. They are reproduced here with the consent of the authors.

Contents

I.   Performance Test A: In re SIA

II.   Selected Answers for Performance Test A

III.   Performance Test B: People v. Draper

IV.   Selected Answers for Performance Test B

July 2013

California Bar Examination

Performance Test A

INSTRUCTIONS AND FILE

IN RE SIA

Instructions . . . .

FILE

Memorandum from Sonia Sanchez to Applicant . . . .

Transcript of Interview with Karen Barber . . . .

Letter from Matt Conyers to Karen Barber . . . .

Complaint to Attorney General on a Nonprofit Organization . . . .

SIA Information Sheet . . . .

SIA Board of Directors Quarterly Meeting Minutes . . . .

IN RE SIA

INSTRUCTIONS

1. This performance test is designed to evaluate your ability to handle a select number of legal authorities in the context of a factual problem involving a client.

2. The problem is set in the fictional State of Columbia, one of the United States.

3. You will have two sets of materials with which to work: a File and a Library.

4. The File contains factual materials about your case. The first document is a memorandum containing the instructions for the tasks you are to complete.

5. The Library contains the legal authorities needed to complete the tasks. The case reports may be real, modified, or written solely for the purpose of this performance test. If the cases appear familiar to you, do not assume that they are precisely the same as you have read before. Read each thoroughly, as if it were new to you. You should assume that cases were decided in the jurisdictions and on the dates shown. In citing cases from the Library, you may use abbreviations and omit page citations.

6. You should concentrate on the materials provided, but you should also bring to bear on the problem your general knowledge of the law. What you have learned in law school and elsewhere provides the general background for analyzing the problem; the File and Library provide the specific materials with which you must work.

7. Although there are no restrictions on how you apportion your time, you should probably allocate at least 90 minutes to reading and organizing before you begin preparing your response.

8. Your response will be graded on its compliance with instructions and on its content, thoroughness, and organization.

SANCHEZ & MARTIN
ATTORNEYS AT LAW

1600 K STREET, SUITE 250
P.O. BOX 423, FRANKLIN, CL 94203-4470
Telephone: (926) 445-2021 Facsimile: (926) 444-3651

MEMORANDUM

TO: Applicant

FROM: Sonia Sanchez

DATE: July 30, 2013

RE: In re SIA

Sensory Integration Alliance, Inc. (SIA) is a nonprofit corporation. Two weeks ago, SIA received a letter from the State Attorney General's Office, enclosing a consumer complaint filed with the Registry of Charitable Trusts. According to the complaint, SIA failed to refund fees for canceled seminars.

As a result of the letter and complaint, SIA's new Executive Director, Karen Barber, did an investigation. To her surprise, she discovered additional serious issues related to the operation of SIA.

Given what she has discovered, Ms. Barber seeks our advice. I need to counsel her concerning what potential liability SIA has for the following acts:

1. Canceled or unscheduled seminars;
2. Payments for Klene Up Kroo janitorial services;
3. Unfiled Form 990s;
4. Expense account reimbursements to Vernon Ellis; and
5. Cruise taken by board members.

Please prepare an objective memorandum that:

    1. For each of the above-listed acts:

        A) States the potential remedies;

        B) States what statute and section prescribes the remedy; and

        C) Discusses whether the available facts would support an effort by the Attorney General to impose the remedy;

and,

    2.   Discusses whether the Attorney General could successfully seek a receivership or dissolution of the corporation.

Another associate is looking at SIA's remedies against the individual transgressors, so do not discuss either SIA's rights against these individuals or the Attorney General's remedies against these individuals.

TRANSCRIPT OF INTERVIEW WITH KAREN BARBER

(July 30, 2013)

SONIA SANCHEZ: Ms. Barber – Karen – from what you told me over the phone, it sounds as if you have some fairly troublesome things you want to talk about. Why don't we go back to the beginning?

KAREN BARBER: Right. First let me say how glad I am that you could see me right away. As I understand it, your firm is counsel to Sensory Integration Alliance, Inc. – SIA.

SANCHEZ: Yes, that's right. We've represented them for the past 10 years or so. I did the original incorporation papers and took care of registering SIA with the Registry of Charitable Trusts. My contact has always been with Vernon Ellis.

BARBER: I'm his replacement. I've just started working as the new Executive Director.

SANCHEZ: When did you start?

BARBER: Two weeks ago.

SANCHEZ: What's your function as Executive Director at SIA?

BARBER: Basically, the same as Vernon Ellis's was. I'm responsible for financial and operational aspects of the corporation and supervising the staff. I report to the five-member Board of Directors, and I work closely with Alan Zackler, the Chair of the Board's Budget and Finance Committee.

SANCHEZ: What happened to Vernon?

BARBER: Unfortunately, about three months ago, he was killed in an auto accident.

SANCHEZ: I'm so sorry to hear that. What is it that brings you here?

BARBER: Well, on my first day of work, I received a letter from the Attorney General's Office enclosing a complaint from a person who claims that she had sent in a check to cover the cost of her attendance at a series of classes that SIA was sponsoring. The Attorney General's letter says I have 30 days to respond. Well, now two weeks.

SANCHEZ: Was the complainant right – that is, did she pay and did she not get a refund?

BARBER: Well, I haven't been able to pinpoint that exactly as yet, but in the course of looking into it, I found something that really looks suspicious. I was – and still am – in the process of getting familiar with the operation, so what I'm going to tell you is what I've found so far.

SANCHEZ: What was suspicious?

BARBER: It's pretty complicated, but let me try to outline it for you. As best I can tell at this point, SIA sponsors seminars and classes on sensory integration several times a year. There's a separate file for each seminar or class, containing spreadsheets showing the names and contact information for each of the people who signed up and recording each person's advance payment. Occasionally, the classes get canceled for one reason or another. When a seminar got canceled, apparently Vernon Ellis sent out letters to the people who had paid telling them of the cancellation and asking whether they wanted a refund or whether they would agree to donate their payment to SIA as a charitable contribution.

SANCHEZ: So, after notice goes out to the public and all arrangements are made, the classes get canceled? Did people who wanted their money back usually get a refund?

BARBER: Well, I found refund checks written to those individuals but when I tried to track them so I could respond to the Attorney General's letter, what I found is that all of those checks had been deposited at Balfour Bank, into an account in Vernon Ellis's name.

SANCHEZ: These were refund checks for <u>all</u> canceled seminars?

BARBER: That's partly right. There are some where all the rooms were booked and instructors engaged and then canceled, apparently because there wasn't enough enrollment. There are about an equal number for which public announcements went out, but as to which I can find absolutely no evidence that anything was ever done to arrange for the events – no rooms booked, no instructors contacted, or anything.

SANCHEZ: You mean nonexistent seminars?

BARBER: Apparently so.

SANCHEZ: Why would anyone do that?

BARBER: Well, here's where it gets complicated. When I moved into Vernon Ellis's office, I was trying to clear out his desk and get mine set up. The three drawers on the right side were locked, and no one knew where the key was. I actually had to call a locksmith to open the drawers. And what I found really surprised me. There were some bank records for an account set up at Balfour Bank in Vernon Ellis's name.

SANCHEZ: I take it that Balfour Bank is not the bank SIA uses for its own accounts, right?

BARBER: Right.

SANCHEZ: Is there any connection between the Balfour Bank records and the "refund" checks that you just told me about?

BARBER: Yes. Here's what I've been able to figure out. As to any person who responded that he wanted his money back, Vernon would write a check in the proper amount payable to that person, then, in what I've been able to recognize as his handwriting, he'd endorse the check with that person's name and deposit it into his account at Balfour Bank. Then, periodically, he would write checks from that account to someone named Adele Stevens, who I've found out is Vernon's sister.

SANCHEZ: Did this pattern appear with respect to the seminars that were canceled after they had actually been planned and also as to the never-planned or "phony" seminars?

BARBER: Pretty much the same.

SANCHEZ: Do you have any idea how much money we're talking about?

BARBER: For the past three years, I've been able to track about $18,000 in refund checks that were written to the paying customers but actually deposited into Vernon Ellis's account at Balfour Bank.

SANCHEZ: On the face of it, it sounds as if Vernon was running a scam. What else did you find in Vernon's desk drawers?

BARBER: There was a whole other series of bank records, and this one is even scarier. There were a series of invoices from a company called The Klene Up Kroo for janitorial services and checks written to that company for the amounts of the invoices. The checks, totaling $22,000 over an 18-month period, were drawn on SIA's account and signed by Vernon Ellis. Those checks were endorsed in the name of Howard Klene and then deposited into an account in Howard Klene's name at First Bank. Regular withdrawals made from the Howard Klene account were then deposited into an account opened in Vernon Ellis's name at Arden Bank. Disbursements from the Arden Bank account were made regularly to Vernon Ellis and Alan Zackler – each of them received cumulatively about $8,000. The current balance in the account is about $6,000.

SANCHEZ: Oh! Is that the same Alan Zackler you report to – a member of SIA's Board and the Chair of the Budget and Finance Committee?

BARBER: I'm certainly assuming so. I mean, I don't know any other Alan Zackler.

SANCHEZ: What else did you find?

BARBER: There's something called a Form 990 that SIA is supposed to file annually with the Attorney General and the Internal Revenue Service.

SANCHEZ: Yes. That's basically an informational tax return for charitable organizations. It includes information such as the major donors, the members of the board, the amounts of compensation paid to board members and staff, and the operational expenses.

BARBER: In the bottom drawer of the desk, there was a file labeled "990s." There were Form 990s that appeared to be completely filled out and signed by Alan Zackler – they were for 2010, 2011, and 2012 and they looked like the originals. Also, memos to the Board from Vernon Ellis, dated the last two years, stating that the 990s for 2010, 2011, and 2012 were timely filed. And there was also a letter from the IRS to Mr. Zackler dated April 20, 2012 stating that the 990s for 2010 and 2011 had never been received by the IRS. On the IRS's letter, there was a handwritten note across the top, "Vernon, please handle this. AZ."

SANCHEZ: Were you able to tell from the forms whether they had been accurately filled out?

BARBER: Not really, but I can tell you that the numbers didn't seem to add up. I mean, I know who the major donors are, and I saw only a few of them listed. Also, the operational expenses reported on the form seemed to me to be overstated quite a bit.

SANCHEZ: What else?

BARBER: One of the folders in the drawer was labeled "Expense Accounts – Vernon/2011." The expense vouchers were filled out in Vernon Ellis's handwriting. A few of them had receipts and other supporting documents attached, but not many. Many entries had to do with SIA travel and entertainment – dinner parties, cocktails, and the like. What I found with respect to a couple of the dinner parties is that Vernon had written an SIA check to the restaurant where the party was held. Then, he'd sometimes attach the restaurant dinner bill to his expense report and get personal reimbursement for it. Also, he would use an SIA credit card, pay the credit card bill with an SIA check, and then also seek personal reimbursement -- double-dipping, so to speak. He got some other reimbursements not supported by receipts. All in all for 2011, the total reimbursement to Vernon was close to $12,500 and only about $4,000 was supported by back-up receipts.

SANCHEZ: Was there any procedure for verifying expense reimbursements and approval of them?

BARBER: As I understand it, expense reports of the Executive Director are supposed to be submitted to the Board of Directors for approval. I checked the board minutes to see if that had been done, and what I found is that Vernon Ellis would attend the board meeting and present his expense reports about once a quarter. The minutes showed that, on each occasion, Alan Zackler "assured the Board" of the accuracy of the expense reports and made a motion that they be accepted as submitted.

SANCHEZ: Is there anything else that gives you pause?

BARBER: While I was going over the check registers, I noticed a $70,000 check written to Wanderly Travel Service. Melanie Wanderly is a member of the Board and she owns Wanderly Travel Service. I tracked it back to an invoice for a Caribbean cruise last summer for the Executive Committee of the Board – the members of the Executive Committee are Alan Zackler and Melanie Wanderly. The Executive Director is an ex officio member of that committee.

SANCHEZ: What was that all about? Do you know?

BARBER: The best I can tell from the records is that Alan Zackler, Melanie Wanderly, and Vernon Ellis and their spouses went on this 10-day cruise. The written agenda described it as a "long-range planning" meeting of the Executive Committee – meeting at breakfast each day for one hour to discuss long-range planning followed by "free time."

SANCHEZ: I agree it sounds suspicious, but maybe not if they really did conduct official business during a substantial portion of the time. Is there any record of what they accomplished by way of long-range planning?

BARBER: None that I could find. In fact, the $70,000 expenditure showed up on the financial statements for that period as "accumulated organizational expenses," and the minutes of that meeting do not show that there was any discussion of the item during Alan Zackler's presentation of the financial report in his capacity as Chair of the Finance and Budget Committee.

SANCHEZ: By the way, what's your sense of the overall financial health of SIA?

BARBER: As far as I can tell, it's pretty healthy. We have a steady stream of charitable donations coming in. We also have a number of foundation grants that are on track for renewal. We also have a half a million dollars in reserves.

SANCHEZ: Well, that's good to hear. I remember reading about problems of charities using commercial fundraisers. Does SIA use any fundraisers?

BARBER: You mean, telemarketers or mass mailers, no, no. We don't do any fundraising appeals to the general public, either on our own or through professional solicitors.

SANCHEZ: How much of this have you disclosed to the Board?

BARBER: Nothing. Fortunately, the Board is changing. The terms of Wanderly and Zackler are up, and they have said that they are stepping down from the SIA Board. At the next meeting, two new board members have been nominated by the other board members, and then new officers and a committee chair will be selected by the new Board.

SANCHEZ: That will make things easier for us to keep this between us for the time being, at least until the next board meeting, and there is a new Board. Our firm represents SIA, not the individual directors. I think there's some exposure here.

BARBER: Well, that's what I want to know. I need to respond to the Attorney General and I'm obviously in a bind.

SANCHEZ: Yes, I agree, and although there are others we probably need to be concerned about, the primary regulator is the State Attorney General. She has broad powers of supervision over charitable organizations like SIA, and there's an extensive statutory scheme for regulations that range from a mere slap on the hands to taking over completely or even dissolving the entity. Given your time constraints, let's focus for now on the Attorney General. I'm going to have to see how all the things you've told me interact with the statutes and what the consequences are. I'll piece it all together and give you written advice.

BARBER: OK. I look forward to hearing from you.

SANCHEZ: I'll be in touch soon. Thanks for coming in.

State of Columbia Department of Justice

1300 I Street, Suite 125
P.O. Box 903447
Franklin, CL 94203-4470

Rosalie Edmonds, Attorney General

July 15, 2013

Karen Barber
Executive Director
Sensory Integration Alliance, Inc.
465 Monument Boulevard, Suite 325
Martinville, CL 93625

    Re: Complaint # 2555

Dear Ms. Barber:

The Registry of Charitable Trusts of our office has received the enclosed complaint regarding an unpaid refund for a seminar sponsored by Sensory Integration Alliance, Inc. and subsequently canceled. We are considering whether to initiate an investigation. Please provide us with an explanation for this problem, state what you intend to do to remedy it, and any other pertinent information. If you do not respond in writing within 30 days, our Investigations Unit will proceed with an investigation.

Sincerely yours,

Matt Conyers
Deputy Attorney General

State of Columbia
DEPARTMENT OF JUSTICE
1300 I Street, Suite 125
P.O. Box 903447
Franklin, CL 94203-4470

Public: (926) 777-3200
Facsimile: (926) 777-4446

COMPLAINT TO ATTORNEY GENERAL
ON A NONPROFIT ORGANIZATION

Name of organization: **Sensory Integration Alliance, Inc.**

List any other names it uses: **Unknown**

Address of organization: **465 Monument Blvd., #325**

City, State, ZIP: **Martinville, CL 93625**

Telephone number of the organization: **(555) 329-4686**

Briefly summarize the main points of your complaint here: (Attach additional pages for the details of your complaint, if necessary.)

I signed up for a 5-session class for $895 that I paid for in advance. I was notified that the classes were canceled and have been promised a refund, but it's been over 6 months and I haven't received a refund yet.

Have charitable funds or other assets been lost, wasted or diverted from proper charitable purposes? Or, is there a danger that such loss will soon occur?   Please explain, giving your best estimate of the amount lost or at risk, if you know:

I have no idea whether the funds have been diverted.

What action has already been taken, either within the organization or with other law enforcement agencies, to try to resolve this problem? Please include dates if available:

I had at least four calls with Vernon Ellis. He assured me that the funds were being refunded, but I never received them.

List the names, addresses and telephone numbers, if known, of all persons you believe may be responsible for this problem:

Unknown

Your name, address and telephone number:

**Alice Rayburn
14 Stonecrest Manor
Jackson, CL
(555) 206-3872**

Date: January 30, 2013

___   Check here, if you request that your identity be kept confidential.

Mail the completed form and any attachments to:

Registry of Charitable Trusts
Office of the Attorney General
P.O. Box 903447
Franklin, CL 94203-4470

Sensory Integration Alliance, Inc.
Research, Education, Accommodation, Treatment
A 501(c)(3) Nonprofit Corporation

Nearly one out of every thousand people has difficulty processing information from one or more of their five basic senses:

- Vision
- Auditory
- Touch
- Olfaction (smell)
- Taste

Plus two lesser-known senses:

- Vestibular (sense of movement)
- Proprioception (sense of position)

The disability includes over-response (for example, when a person finds the touch of clothing or physical contact unbearable) and under-response (for example, when a person shows little or no reaction to pain or temperature extremes).

Sensory Integration Alliance, Inc. (SIA) exists to help people who live with sensory disorders and their families.

Services to Individuals with Sensory Disabilities

Information - SIA collects and disseminates up-to-date information to enable individuals to understand their disability, to find treatment, and to seek accommodations at school or in the workplace. This information is available on the SIA website, www.senses.org.

Referral - SIA maintains a database of medical and education specialists and is able to make referrals for individuals to receive the services necessary and appropriate for their condition.

Services to Families of Individuals with Sensory Disabilities

Education - SIA convenes presentations and seminars to explain sensory integration disorder (SID) and its treatments, therapies, and other interventions to parents and other family members. Seminars feature qualified professionals, doctors, occupational therapists, psychologists, educators, etc. Topics include new therapies, special education programs at schools, available community resources and more.

Services to Professionals

Education - SIA will convene presentations and seminars to bring the latest information to professionals working in the field of sensory disability. Seminars will feature expert practitioners and researchers. Topics may include new therapies, special education programs at schools, available community resources, and more.

Referrals - Professionals have the opportunity to be part of SIA's referral network. Please contact Karen Barber, SIA Executive Director, for details. kbarber@senses.org.

Minutes of the Quarterly Meeting, SIA Board of Directors

September 15, 2011

The meeting was convened at 5:00 p.m. at the SIA offices. All board members were present, and the Chair declared that a quorum was present.

Moved, seconded and resolved to approve the minutes of the June 6, 2011 meeting.

Executive Director, Vernon Ellis, provided his report to the Board. Director Alan Zackler orally presented his Budget and Finance Committee Report, concluding that the financial status of SIA was solid, and asked that the Board approve all of the expense reimbursements of the previous quarter. Directors Jeff Garcia and Warrick Dunne questioned certain expenditures. Director Zackler responded that he had reviewed each of them and that each was bona fide. The Board moved, seconded and resolved approval of payment of the quarterly expenditures.

The Board discussed the status of the public seminars. Executive Director Ellis reported that the programs were on track and had been well received.

The meeting was adjourned at 5:45 p.m.

Minutes of the Quarterly Meeting, SIA Board of Directors

April 15, 2012

The meeting was convened at 5:15 p.m. at the SIA offices. All board members were present, and the Chair declared that a quorum was present.

Moved, seconded and resolved to approve the minutes of the January 15, 2012 meeting.

Director Alan Zackler orally presented his Budget and Finance Committee Report, and reported that expenditures were under the budgeted amounts and that revenues were on target. Director Warrick Dunne led a discussion by several directors about the apparent increase in staff travel reimbursements. Director Zackler explained that these were legitimate expenses associated with the increase in public seminar programs, and that all of the expenditures had been reviewed and each was well-documented in the files of SIA.

The meeting was adjourned at 5:45 p.m.

Minutes of the Quarterly Meeting, SIA Board of Directors

January 15, 2013

The meeting was convened at 5:00 p.m. at the SIA offices. All board members were present, and the Chair declared that a quorum was present.

Moved, seconded and resolved to approve the minutes of the September 15, 2012 meeting.

Director Alan Zackler reported that preparation of the annual budget had been delayed because all of the previous year's income and expense data were not ready. Executive Director Vernon Ellis was still working on it. Several directors expressed serious concern. Director Zackler reassured them that everything was in order; just a little slow this year. Director Jeff Garcia asked if SIA's reports to the IRS and State Franchise Tax Board had been filed, and Director Zackler assured the Board that all reporting requirements had been met.

The meeting was adjourned at 5:45 p.m.

July 2013

California
Bar
Examination

Performance Test A

LIBRARY

IN RE SIA

LIBRARY

Selected Provisions of the Columbia Corporations Code,
Nonprofit Corporation Law . . . .

Selected Provisions of the Columbia Government Code,
also known as the Columbia Uniform Supervision of
Trustees for Charitable Purposes Act (the Uniform Act) . . . .

People v. Orange County Charitable Services
Columbia Court of Appeal (1998) . . . .

Attorney General v. Sidley Memorial Hospital
Columbia Supreme Court (1994) . . . .

Selected Provisions of the Columbia Corporations Code, Nonprofit Corporation Law

Section 5231.

(a) A director shall perform the duties of a director, including duties as a member of any committee of the board upon which the director may serve, in good faith, in a manner such director believes to be in the best interests of the corporation and with such care, including reasonable inquiry, as an ordinarily prudent person in a like position would use under similar circumstances.

(b) In performing the duties of a director, a director shall be entitled to rely on information, opinions, reports or statements, including financial statements and other financial data, in each case prepared or presented by:

(1) One or more officers or employees of the corporation whom the director believes to be reliable and competent in the matters presented;

(2) Counsel, independent accountants, or other persons as to matters which the director believes to be within such person's professional or expert competence; or

(3) A committee of the board upon which the director does not serve, as to matters within its designated authority, which committee the director believes to merit confidence, so long as, in any such case, the director acts in good faith, after reasonable inquiry when the need therefor is indicated by the circumstances and without knowledge that would cause such reliance to be unwarranted.

(c) Except as provided in Section 5233, a person who performs the duties of a director in accordance with subdivisions (a) and (b) shall have no liability based upon any alleged failure to discharge the person's obligations as a director, including, without limiting the generality of the foregoing, any actions or omissions which exceed or defeat a public or charitable purpose to which a corporation, or assets held by it, are dedicated.

Section 5233.

(a)   Except as provided in subdivision (b), for the purpose of this section, a self-dealing transaction means a transaction to which the corporation is a party and in which one or more of its directors has a material financial interest and which does not meet the requirements of subdivision (d). Such a director is an "interested director" for the purpose of this section.

(b)   The provisions of this section do not apply to any of the following:

(1) An action of the board fixing the compensation of a director as a director or officer of the corporation.

(2) A transaction which is part of a public or charitable program of the corporation if it: (i) is approved or authorized by the corporation in good faith and without unjustified favoritism; and (ii) results in a benefit to one or more directors or their families because they are in the class of persons intended to be benefited by the public or charitable program.

(3) A transaction, of which the interested director or directors have no actual knowledge, and which does not exceed the lesser of 1 percent of the gross receipts of the corporation for the preceding fiscal year, or one hundred thousand dollars ($100,000).

(c)   The Attorney General may bring an action in the superior court of the proper county for the remedies specified in subdivision (e).

(d)   In any action brought under subdivision (c) the remedies specified in subdivision (e) shall not be granted if the following facts are established:

(1) The corporation entered into the transaction for its own benefit;

(2) The transaction was fair and reasonable as to the corporation at the time the corporation entered into the transaction;

(3) Prior to consummating the transaction, the board authorized or approved the transaction in good faith by a vote of a majority of the directors then in office without counting the vote of the interested director or directors, and with knowledge of the material facts concerning the transaction and the director's interest in the transaction; and,

(4) Prior to consummating the transaction in good faith, determined after reasonable investigation under the circumstances that: (i) the corporation could not have obtained a more advantageous arrangement with reasonable effort under the circumstances, or (ii) the corporation in fact could not have obtained a more advantageous arrangement with reasonable effort under the circumstances.

(e)   If a self-dealing transaction has taken place, the interested director or directors shall do such things and pay such damages as in the discretion of the court will provide an equitable and fair remedy to the corporation, taking into account any benefit received by the corporation and whether the interested director or directors acted in good faith and with intent to further the best interest of the corporation. Without limiting the generality of the foregoing, the court may order the director to do any or all of the following:

(1) Account for any profits made from such transaction, and pay them to the corporation;

(2) Pay the corporation the value of the use of any of its property used in such transaction; and

(3) Return or replace any property lost to the corporation as a result of such transaction, together with any income or appreciation lost to the corporation by reason of such transaction, or account for any proceeds of sale of such property, and pay the proceeds to the corporation together with interest at the legal rate. In addition, the court may, in its discretion, grant exemplary damages for a fraudulent or malicious violation of this section.

Section 5250.

A corporation is subject at all times to examination by the Attorney General, on behalf of the State, to ascertain the condition of its affairs and to what extent, if at all, it fails to comply with trusts which it has assumed, or has departed from the purposes for which it is formed. In case of any such failure or departure, the Attorney General may institute, in the name of the State, the proceeding necessary to correct the noncompliance or departure.

Section 6511.

(a)   The Attorney General may bring an action against any corporation or purported corporation, in the name of the people of this State, upon the Attorney General's own information or upon complaint of a private party, to procure a judgment dissolving the corporation and annulling, vacating or forfeiting its corporate existence upon any of the following grounds:

(1) The corporation has seriously offended against any provision of the statutes regulating corporations or charitable organizations.

(2) The corporation has fraudulently abused or usurped corporate privileges or powers.

(3) The corporation has violated any provision of law by any act or default which under the law is a ground for forfeiture of corporate existence.

(b)   If the ground of the action is a matter or act which the corporation has done or omitted to do that can be corrected by amendment of its articles or by other corporate action, such suit shall not be maintained unless: (1) the Attorney General, at least 30 days prior to the institution of suit, has given the corporation written notice of the matter or act done or omitted to be done; and (2) the corporation has failed to institute proceedings to correct it within the 30-day period, or thereafter fails to duly and properly make such amendment or take the corrective corporate action.

(c)   In any such action, the court may order restitutionary and/or injunctive relief to compensate or protect members of the public who have been harmed by the corporation's violations of the law. The court may order dissolution or such other or partial relief as it deems just and expedient. The court also may appoint a receiver for winding up the affairs of the corporation or may order that the corporation be wound up by its board, subject to the supervision of the court.

Selected Provisions of the Columbia Government Code, also known as the Columbia Uniform Supervision of Trustees for Charitable Purposes Act (the Uniform Act)

Section 125.

(a) Annually, every charitable corporation, unincorporated association, and trustee subject to this article shall file with the Attorney General a copy of the Form 990 submitted to the Internal Revenue Service.

(b) Upon registration, a corporation shall file the first Form 990 not later than four months and 15 days following the close of the first calendar or fiscal year in which property is initially received.

(c) In addition to a registration fee, a charitable corporation or trustee, or commercial fundraiser may be assessed a late fee of twenty-five dollars ($25) for each month or part of the month it fails to file its first and subsequent Form 990s.

Section 126.

(a) Any person who violates any provision of this Act with intent to deceive or defraud any charity or individual is liable for a civil penalty not exceeding ten thousand dollars ($10,000).

(b) Except as provided in subdivision (d), any person who violates any other provision of this Act is liable for a civil penalty, as follows:

(1) For the first offense, a fine not exceeding one thousand dollars ($1,000).

(2) For any subsequent offense, a fine not exceeding two thousand five hundred dollars ($2,500).

(c) Any offense committed under this Act involving a solicitation may be deemed to have been committed at either the place at which the solicitation was initiated or at the place where the solicitation was received.

(d) Any person who violates only subdivision (a) or (b) of Section 125 shall not be liable for a civil penalty under subdivision (b) if the person: (1) has not received reasonable notice of the violation; and (2) has not been given a reasonable opportunity to correct the violation. The Attorney General shall notify in writing a person who violates only subdivisions (a) or (b) of Section 125 that he or she has 30 days to correct the violation.

(e)   The recovery of a civil penalty pursuant to this section precludes assessment of a late fee pursuant to Section 125 for the same offense.

Section 127.

(a)   The primary responsibility for supervising charitable trusts in Columbia, for ensuring compliance with trusts and articles of incorporation, and for protection of assets held by charitable trusts and public benefit corporations, resides in the Attorney General. The Attorney General has broad powers under common law and Columbia statutory law to carry out these charitable trust enforcement responsibilities. These powers include, but are not limited to, charitable trust enforcement actions under all of the following:

(1) This Act;

(2) The Nonprofit Corporation Law, Corporations Code sections 5000, et. seq.

(b)   The Attorney General may refuse to register or may revoke or suspend the registration of a charitable corporation or trustee or commercial fundraiser whenever the Attorney General finds that the charitable corporation or trustee or commercial fundraiser has violated or is operating in violation of any provisions of this Act.

People v. Orange County Charitable Services

Columbia Court of Appeal (1998)

This appeal arises from a case brought by the Attorney General against more than 130 individual and business entities engaged in commercial fundraising, and related charitable organizations. After a bench trial, the court entered a judgment enjoining the defendants from engaging in the business of soliciting funds for charitable purposes until they had made a complete accounting of nearly $15 million in funds raised from the public through telephone solicitations. The court further enjoined them from making false or misleading statements in their solicitations and directed them to make specific, statutorily mandated affirmative disclosures. It also imposed a constructive charitable trust on the funds.

The appellant, Mitchell Doyle, dba Orange County Charitable Services, the only party pursuing this appeal, challenges the court's factual findings as unsupported by sufficient evidence and its legal conclusions as erroneous. We affirm.

Orange County Charitable Services (OCCS) is a sole proprietorship established by Mitchell Doyle (Doyle) in 1987. It is in the business of raising funds for charities through telephone solicitations for contributions from members of the public. In the years 1990 through 1994, OCCS was registered as a commercial fundraiser, as required under Columbia's Uniform Supervision of Trustees for Charitable Purposes Act (the Uniform Act), Government Code sections 125, et. seq.

In order to increase OCCS's profitability, Doyle created charities that would contract their fundraising with OCCS, American Veterans Assistance (AVA) and Columbians Against Drugs (CAD). He then hired OCCS to raise funds for both charities. AVA and CAD agreed to pay OCCS 92 percent and 93 percent, respectively, of the gross revenues secured by the fundraiser.

Doyle controlled the finances and, to a significant degree, the operations of AVA and CAD from their inception dates. The charities were incorporated as Columbia public benefit corporations. Each charity's articles of incorporation contained substantially the following clause: "This corporation is a nonprofit public benefit corporation and is not organized for the private gain of any person. This corporation is organized and operated exclusively for charitable purposes within the meaning of Section 501(c)(3) of the Internal Revenue Code. The property of this corporation is irrevocably dedicated to charitable purposes and no part of the net income or assets of this corporation shall ever inure to the benefit of any director, officer, or member or to the benefit of any private person."

OCCS entered into more than 100 subcontracts with various parties to conduct commercial fundraising for various charities, including AVA and CAD. Under the customary subcontract, 10 percent or less of the gross revenues would be paid to the charitable organizations. The subcontractor and OCCS divided the 90 percent fee, according to the terms of the agreement.

OCCS operated telemarketing rooms -- "boiler rooms" -- throughout the state. The boiler room managers were instructed to have telemarketers inform the donors that 75 to 80 percent of the money being raised was used for "program services." OCCS gave similar instructions to its subcontractors. Telemarketers identified themselves as "from the charity." After donors agreed to contribute, the monies were collected by the fundraiser and deposited into the respective charitable organization's bank account. Interestingly, AVA and CAD were not accused of any wrongdoing. Apparently, the meager 7 to 8 percent of monies redounding to the charities was actually used for charitable purposes. Were it otherwise, the Attorney General could well have sought similar injunctive and other relief against the charitable organizations, their board members, and any employees who committed any wrongdoing.

Numerous donor witnesses testified regarding misrepresentations. Typical testimony recounted multiple telephone solicitations between 1991 and 1994 in which the telemarketers identified themselves as being *from* the charities. No one ever disclosed his or her commercial fundraising status. No one was informed about the percentage of funds that would be used to pay for the fundraising.

Public benefit corporations and commercial fundraisers must file annual reports, containing specific forms and information, with the Attorney General. Among these reports is a copy of the Form 990, an informational tax return filed with the Internal Revenue Service (IRS) annually. The Form 990 contains information about sources and amounts of income, salaries for key employees, a list of board members and their compensation, and the top five consultant fees. OCCS filed no statutory financial reports of its fundraising for charitable purposes for the calendar year 1993. OCCS registered as a commercial fundraiser in Columbia for each of the years 1990 through 1994. The 1990 reports did not mention OCCS's fundraising activities. Instead, they reported figures copied from the annual federal informational tax returns (Form 990s) of AVA and CAD. Reports for subsequent years either were copied from the charities' Form 990s or set forth figures which were utterly irreconcilable with the charities' own reporting. For instance, while OCCS reported it raised only $242,640 for CAD in 1991, CAD reported it received more than $400,000 from OCCS that same year.

In its statement of decision, the court found, inter alia:

The defendants conducted their business unlawfully;

The defendants raised money for restricted charitable purposes. The funds were impressed with a restricted charitable trust, but defendants failed to keep separate accounts of the funds, did not use them for the specified purposes, and, in fact, used them for other purposes; and

OCCS failed to file an accounting of fundraising activities for charities in 1993. Its inaccurate reports of activities in 1990, 1991 and 1992 contained multimillion-dollar discrepancies.

In its eight-page judgment, the court enjoined appellants from making various false or misleading representations to prospective donors, directed them to make specified affirmative representations, barred them from soliciting for organizations which had not authorized them to do so, imposed certain reporting duties on appellants, and directed them to account for their fundraising activities in Columbia up to the date of the judgment, including a full accounting for all funds received by them in the name of 11 different charitable programs. The court further enjoined appellants from commercial fundraising pending a complete accounting, and ordered them to register as commercial fundraisers and maintain all required bonds. It also imposed a charitable trust on monies recovered under the accounting provisions of the judgment. It imposed civil penalties against a number of individual defendants that were authorized under various statutes, based on violations of financial reporting obligations.

Virtually every aspect of the activities of charities and their commercial fundraisers is subject to comprehensive regulation. The assets of nonprofit corporations such as AVA and CAD, organized solely for charitable purposes, are impressed with a charitable trust which the Attorney General has a duty to protect. A complete range of equitable remedies vindicates the public interest in charitable assets; such remedies include injunctions to prevent and correct breach of fiduciary obligations arising from a trust.

Under the Uniform Act, commercial fundraisers for charitable purposes must register with the Attorney General and file financial reports of the money they raise for charities in Columbia and their fundraising costs. Government Code section 125. A commercial fundraiser for charitable purposes is defined as any individual, corporation, or legal entity who, for compensation, solicits funds in Columbia for charitable purposes or, as a result of a solicitation, receives or controls the funds. Commercial fundraisers are "constructive trustees" with respect to the funds they raise, and they have an affirmative, unqualified duty to report to the Attorney General. Commercial fundraisers must disclose to persons solicited, upon written or oral request, the percentage of the funds that goes to fundraising expenses. The fundraiser who fails to comply with the registration and financial reporting requirements of the statute may not solicit funds for charitable purposes, and failure to comply is grounds for an injunction against solicitation in this state for charitable purposes and other civil remedies provided by law.

The Attorney General's broad common law powers to oversee charities extends far beyond the Uniform Act. Under provisions of the Nonprofit Corporation Law, the Attorney General may obtain restitutionary relief and injunctive relief, and the remedies are cumulative to those available under other provisions of the law. Corporations Code section 6511.

A high hurdle must be overcome by appellants challenging the sufficiency of evidence. Where, as here, the court issues a statement of decision, it need only recite ultimate facts supporting the judgment being entered. The court's decision was supported by substantial evidence.

Appellant further contends the court misinterpreted Columbia's charitable trust laws and the fiduciary responsibilities of charitable trustees and went "well beyond any statutory authority" in its judgment. We are not persuaded.

The judgment is affirmed.

Attorney General v. Sidley Memorial Hospital

Columbia Supreme Court (1994)

The Attorney General filed suit against Sidley Memorial Hospital (Sidley), a Columbia charitable corporation, seeking its dissolution or, in the alternative, the appointment of a monitor to manage its day-to-day operations, subject to supervision by the trial court until the court should deem such supervision no longer needed. After a bench trial, the court entered judgment ordering Sidley's dissolution and putting in place a receiver to wind up its affairs. Sidley appealed. We now reverse the judgment and remand the matter to the trial court with directions to appoint a monitor.

The Attorney General brought this action, contending that various past and present members of Sidley's Board of Directors conspired to enrich themselves and certain financial institutions with which they were affiliated by favoring those institutions in financial dealings with Sidley, and that they breached their fiduciary duties of care and loyalty in the management of Sidley's funds. The complaint alleged violations of the Columbia Corporations Code, and violations of the Columbia Uniform Supervision of Trustees for Charitable Purposes Act. The evidence presented at trial told the following story.

In 1980, Sidley's Board of Directors revised the corporate bylaws in preparation for an expected increase in the volume and complexity of its operations following construction of a new building. Under the new bylaws, the Board was to consist of from 25 to 35 trustees, who were to meet at least twice each year. Between such meetings, an Executive Committee was to represent the Board, and was authorized, inter alia, to open checking and savings accounts, approve Sidley's budget, renew mortgages, and enter into contracts. A Finance Committee was created to review the budget and to report regularly on the amount of cash available for investment. Management of those investments was to be supervised by an Investment Committee, which was to work closely with the Finance Committee in such matters.

In fact, until 1988, Sidley's management was handled almost exclusively by two directors who were also officers: Dr. Adele Orem, Sidley's Administrator, and Mr. Lloyd Ernst, its Treasurer. Unlike most of their fellow directors, to whom membership on the Sidley Board was a charitable service incidental to their principal vocations, Orem and

Ernst were continuously involved on almost a daily basis in Sidley's affairs. They dominated the Board and its Executive Committee, which routinely accepted their recommendations and ratified their actions. Even more significantly, neither the Finance Committee nor the Investment Committee ever met or conducted business from the date of their creation until 1991, three years after the death of Dr. Orem. As a result, budgetary and investment decisions during this period, like most other management decisions affecting Sidley's finances, were handled by Orem and Ernst, receiving only cursory supervision from the Executive Committee and the full Board.

Dr. Orem's death obliged some of the other directors to play a more active role in running Sidley. The Executive Committee, and particularly Stacy Reed, as Chairman of the Board, President, and ex officio member of the Executive Committee, became more deeply involved in the day-to-day management while efforts were made to find a new Administrator. The person who was eventually selected for that office, Dr. Ralph Jarvis, had little managerial experience and his performance was not entirely satisfactory. Mr. Ernst still made most of the financial and investment decisions for Sidley, but his actions and failures to act came slowly under increasing scrutiny by several of the other directors.

Prompted by these difficulties, Mr. Reed decided to activate the Finance and Investment Committee in 1991. However, as Chairman of the Finance Committee and member of the Investment Committee as well as Treasurer, Mr. Ernst continued to exercise dominant control over investment decisions and, on several occasions, discouraged and flatly refused to respond to inquiries by other directors into such matters. It was only after the death of Mr. Ernst in 1992 that the other directors appear to have assumed an identifiable supervisory role over investment policy and Sidley's fiscal management in general.

Presented with this evidence, the trial court decided that dissolution of Sidley was appropriate. The court recognized that such a result was harsh, but stated that it believed that equity required the outcome in light of what it believed to be Sidley's abandonment of its charitable purpose in favor of allowing itself to become the acquiescent instrument of Dr. Orem and Mr. Ernst.

A decision by the trial court to dissolve a charitable corporation is reviewed for abuse of discretion. *Attorney General v. The Children's Trust* (Col. Supreme Ct., 1971). For the reasons that follow, we find that the trial court erred under that standard.

The function of equity is not to punish, but merely to take such action as may be necessary to prevent the recurrence of improper conduct. Where voluntary action has been taken in good faith to minimize such recurrence, this is a factor which the court can take into account in formulating relief.

In attempting to balance the equities under the circumstances shown by the record, there are factors that lead us to believe that dissolution of Sidley is not necessary. First, it is clear that the practices criticized by the Attorney General have, to a considerable extent, been corrected and that the directors who were principally responsible for lax handling of funds have died. Second, there is no indication that any of the other directors were involved in fraudulent practices or profited personally by lapses in proper fiscal supervision, and, indeed, the overall operation of Sidley in terms of low costs, efficient services, and quality patient care has been superior.

We are well aware that Sidley must take proper steps to insure a clean and final break between the past and the future. A recent greater awareness of past laxity is encouraging. To help it complete the task, the trial court should appoint a monitor to manage its day-to-day operations, subject to supervision until it may deem such supervision no longer needed. We remand the matter to that court with directions to do so.

Reversed and remanded.

SELECTED ANSWER 1

MEMORANDUM

TO: Sonia Sanchez
FROM: Applicant
DATE: July 30, 2013
RE: In re SIA

You have asked me to prepare an objective memorandum that discusses the potential remedies that the Attorney General (AG) could seek against SIA for five acts: cancelled or unscheduled seminars, payments for Klene Up Kroo janitorial services; unfiled Form 990s, expense account reimbursements to Vernon Ellis, and a cruise taken by board members. In addition, you asked me to discuss whether the AG could successfully seek a dissolution or a receivership of SIA.

SIA's Potential Liability

1. Cancelled or Unscheduled Seminars

Potential Remedies and Supporting Statutes

The AG has broad discretion to institute actions necessary to correct a charitable corporation's noncompliance with or departure from the trusts that the corporation has assumed and the purposes for which it was formed. Nonprofit Corporation Law Section 5250. The AG has broad powers under common and statutory law to carry out her charitable enforcement responsibilities. Uniform Act section 127(a). The AG may dispose of "[a] complete range of equitable remedies [to] vindicate the public interest in charitable assets" including "injunctions to prevent and correct breach of fiduciary obligations arising from a trust." *People v. Orange County Charitable Services*, (Col. Ct. App. 1998).

Beyond the statutory powers created by the Uniform Act, the Nonprofit Corporation Law contains broad common law powers that are cumulative to other remedies available under other provisions of the law. *Orange County Charitable Services*. A court may order "restitutionary and/or injunctive relief to compensate or protect members of the public who have been harmed by the corporation's violations of the law." Nonprofit Corporation Law Section 6511(c).

The remedies available under the Uniform Act and the Nonprofit Corporation Law have been broadly construed to include injunctions against engaging in specified activities, the imposition of reporting requirements, requirements to provide a full accounting of funds, the imposition of civil penalties, and the imposition of a constructive trust. *Orange County Charitable Services*.

With respect to the cancelled or unscheduled seminars, the AG might seek to impose an injunction halting the offering of seminars, restitution to individuals who sought and did not receive refunds, a full accounting of funds received for cancelled or unscheduled seminars, and the imposition of a constructive trust on monies recovered as a result of the accounting. See Nonprofit Corporation Law Section 6511(c); Uniform Act 127(c); *Orange County Charitable Services*.

Whether Facts Would Support Effort to Impose a Remedy
On July 15, 2013, the AG sent SIA a notice that its office had received a complaint regarding an unpaid refund for a cancelled seminar. Alice Rayburn had sent in a complaint to the AG stating that she had paid $895 for a class that subsequently was cancelled. Despite requesting a refund on at least four occasions, Rayburn has not received a refund in over six months.

Karen Barber, the newly-appointed Executive Director at SIA, has found indications that when seminars were cancelled, the prior Executive Director, Vernon Ellis, would send letters to individuals who had paid asking whether they wanted a refund or whether they were willing to make their payment a donation to SIA. When individuals requested a refund, Ellis would make out a check to them, but deposit the check in his own account at Balfour Bank. Checks from the account at Balfour Bank were then written to Ellis's sister, Adele Stevens. A similar pattern of events occurred when seminars were publicly announced, but never actually planned. Approximately $18,000 in refund checks were deposited into Ellis's account in the past three years.

A court is likely to find that SIA has failed to comply with the trust it assumed or departed from the purposes for which it had been formed with respect to the cancelled or unscheduled seminars. Nonprofit Corporation Law Section 5250. As SIA's information sheet states, one of SIA's core services is to convene presentations and seminars to explain sensory integration disorder and its treatments to parents and family members and to provide updated information and research to professionals in the field. In cancelling a number of seminars and in failing even to schedule or plan others, SIA has been failing to comply with its trust or fulfill its purposes. Accordingly, the AG is empowered to initiate any proceeding necessary to correct SIA's noncompliance and departure. Nonprofit Corporation Law Section 5250.

In this case, a court likely will impose restitutionary relief to benefit those individuals, such as Rayburn, who requested but did not receive a refund. Nonprofit Corporation Law Section 6511(c). In addition, the facts suggest that other individuals may not have requested a refund, but instead made their payment a donation to SIA. This situation is somewhat similar to *People v. Orange County Charitable Services*. In that case, the court found that the defendant, a corporation that ostensibly raised money for charitable purposes, actually had failed to keep accounts of funds raised or to use them for specified purposes. In that case, the court ordered a full accounting of funds raised by the defendant and imposed a charitable trust on all monies recovered as part of the accounting. The court noted that had the charities involved not actually used the funds actually raised for charitable purposes, they might have been subject to similar injunctions and other relief. Similarly, here, SIA has collected funds for the purposes of holding seminars that were never actually held or planned, and therefore the funds that were raised were not actually used for the charitable purposes for which they were intended. The court likely will order an accounting for all the funds raised for the purposes of holding seminars and impose a constructive trust on any funds raised but not refunded. Those funds might then be used to provide restitution to individuals harmed by SIA's violation of the law. Nonprofit Corporation Law Section 6511(c).

In *Orange County Charitable Services*, the court also enjoined the defendant from undertaking further commercial fundraising pending a complete accounting and barred the defendant from making misleading or false representations to prospective donors. Similarly, here, a court likely would bar SIA from advertising seminars pending an accounting and might enjoin SIA from scheduling seminars without actually planning or holding them.

2.   Payments for Klene Up Kroo Janitorial Services

Potential Remedies and Supporting Statutes

A member of a charitable corporation's board of directors has a fiduciary obligation to avoid self-dealing transactions, that is, a transaction to which a corporation is a party and in which a director has a material financial interest. Nonprofit Corporation Law Section 5223(a), (e). If a self-interested transaction has taken place, the interested director may be required to pay compensation to the corporation. Nonprofit Corporation Law Section 5223(e).

As described above, the AG has broad equitable powers to ensure a charitable corporation's compliance with its trust. The AG has a "complete range of equitable remedies" at her disposal, and these include "injunctions to prevent and correct breach of fiduciary obligations arising from a trust." *Orange County Charitable Services*. Here, the AG might seek an injunction to prevent further payments to the Klene Up Kroo (KUK) and might seek an accounting of all payments made to KUK.

Facts Supporting Remedies

In this case, SIA appears to have paid KUK $22,000 over an 18-month period. Those checks were deposited into an account in Howard Klene's name, and then regular withdrawals were made to an account in Ellis's name at Arden Bank. Disbursements were then made from the Arden Bank account to Ellis and Alan Zackler, the Chair of

SIA's Budget and Finance Committee. It appears, at the very least, that a self-interested transaction occurred that benefitted Ellis and Zackler. There are no indications that an exception occurred – for example, the transaction was not compensation for either Ellis or Zackler, it was not a charitable purpose of SIA, and the contention that Ellis and Zackler were unaware of transfers in the amount of a total of $16,000 strains credulity. See Uniform Act Section 5233(b). Nor does it appear that the transaction was authorized by the board with knowledge of the material facts. Indeed, based on the Board meeting minutes the board appears to have relied solely on Zackler's assurances that expenditures were reasonable and legitimate. See Nonprofit Corporation Law Section 5231.

The AG's broad equitable powers would likely extend to an injunction barring SIA from further dealings with KUK or other self-interested transactions. In addition, the AG could likely obtain an accounting of all payments to KUK from SIA to permit the AG to pursue actions against the individual officers involved and to ensure that no further payments are made. Also, the AG might successfully seek a monitor, as discussed below in the section regarding the expense account reimbursements.

3.   Unfiled Form 990s

Potential Remedies and Supporting Statutes
Every charitable corporation is required to file Form 990s annually with the Internal Revenue Service and to file a copy with the AG. Uniform Act Section 125(a). Form 990s include information about sources of income, salaries of key employees, board members and compensation, and consultant fees. *OCCS*.

The AG has the authority to seek civil penalties for the failure to file Form 990s. Uniform Act Section 125, 126(a), (b). If the failure to file the Form 990s was done with the intent to deceive or defraud, the civil penalty may be in an amount not to exceed $10,000. Uniform Act Section 126(a). Otherwise, the fine for a first offense is not to exceed $1,000 and the fine for any subsequent offense is not to exceed $2,500. Civil penalties may not be imposed where the trust has not received reasonable notice of the violation and has not been given a reasonable opportunity to correct the violation. Uniform Act Section 126(d). In addition, the AG shall notify in writing a person who fails to file Form 990s that he or she has 30 days to correct the violation. *Id.*

The AG may also assess a late fee of $25 per month for each month or part of a month that an organization fails to file Form 990s. Uniform Act Section 125(c). However, if the AG seeks a civil penalty, she may not also assess a late fee for the same offense. Uniform Act Section 126(e).

The AG may also refuse to register or may suspend or revoke the registration of any charitable corporation that has violated a provision of the Uniform Act, including a charitable corporation that has failed to file required Form 990s. Uniform Act Section 127(b).

Facts Supporting Remedies

According to Barber, original Form 990s for the years 2010, 2011, and 2012 were found in Ellis's desk. In addition, Ellis had sent memos to the Board indicating that the forms for those years had been timely filed. Zackler also assured the Board at the January 15, 2013 meeting that all reporting requirements, including IRS reporting requirements, had been met.

Despite this, Barber also found a letter from the IRS to Zackler indicating that Form 990s for 2010 and 2011 had not been received by the IRS. The letter had a handwritten note from Zackler asking Ellis to handle it. In addition, Barber reports that the Forms she found did not appear to list all of the major donors and appeared to contain overstated operational expenses.

It is not entirely clear based on these facts whether the required Form 990s actually were provided either to the IRS or to the AG. It is possible that the forms were filed after the letter from the IRS was received. In addition, the AG has not sent SIA a notification of a failure to file required Form 990s. Prior to seeking civil penalties, the

AG will have to send a notification giving SIA 30 days to correct the deficiency. Uniform Act Section 126(d).

However, if it is the case, as it appears to be, that the Form 990s for 2010 and 2011 have not been filed as required, the AG likely could seek penalties after giving SIA an opportunity to correct the deficiency. In addition, there are facts from which the court could find that the failure to report was made with the intent to deceive or defraud. It appears that the Board has been misled about SIA's compliance with reporting requirements and the forms appear to have been filled out incorrectly. The AG could make a strong case that the higher civil penalty of up to $10,000 is warranted. Uniform Act 126(a).

In addition, if the AG does not seek the higher penalty, the AG likely will be able to recover up to $1000 for the failure to file the 2010 990 and up to $2500 for the failure to file the 2011 990. SIA received reasonable notice of the violation when the IRS sent a notification that it had not received the forms and also has had more than two years to correct that failure. Uniform Act Section 126(d). In the alternative, the AG could seek late fees in the amount of $25 for every late month, of $300 per year, for a total of $900 for the 2010 form and $600 for the 2011 form.

The AG might also seek to revoke or suspend SIA's registration for its failure to file the required forms. Uniform Act Section 127(b).

4. Expense Account Reimbursements to Vernon Ellis

Remedies Available and Statutes
A director is required to act in the best interests of the corporation and to take such care as a reasonably prudent person would in conducting his or her own business. Nonprofit Corporation Law Section 5231(a). Directors can rely on statements presented by an officer or employee whom the director believes to be reliable, or a committee of the board on which the director does not serve as to matters in its authority as long as the director acts in good faith after reasonable inquiry and without knowledge of proprieties.

Nonprofit Corporation Law Section 5231(b). If a director complies with that duty, he is shielded from liability. Nonprofit Corporation Law Section 5231(c).

However, as described above, the AG has broad equitable powers to ensure a charitable corporation's compliance with its trust. Nonprofit Corporation Law Section 5250. The AG has a "complete range of equitable remedies" at her disposal, and these include "injunctions to prevent and correct breach of fiduciary obligations arising from a trust." *Orange County Charitable Services*. These include the ability to seek any partial relief from a court for violations of trust duties that may be equitable. Nonprofit Corporations Law Section 6115(c).

With respect to the expense account reimbursements to Ellis, the AG might seek to impose reporting and accounting requirements on SIA for all expenses paid out to officers and board members, might appoint a monitor to supervise SIA's day-to-day operations subject to supervision, and might enjoin further expense account reimbursements without authorization from a monitor.

Facts Supporting Remedies

Barber has reported that Ellis essentially double-billed for expenses to SIA. When paying for travel and entertainment, Ellis would use SIA funds and then, separately, submit the check or bill for personal reimbursement. In addition, Ellis was reimbursed for approximately $12,500 in expenses in 2011, only $4,000 of which was supported by receipts. Although some members of the Board expressed some discomfort, on September 15, 2011, the Board accepted the assurances of Zackler, the chair of the budget and finance committee, that the expenditures were bona fide.

Although it likely is the case that the Board was entitled to rely on the representations of Zackler so as to escape personal liability, see Nonprofit Corporations Law Section 5231(b), (c), nevertheless, the failure to appropriately audit expense accounts and to ensure that only valid reimbursements are made would likely permit the AG to seek a monitor to ensure that similar improper conduct does not occur in the future. In *Attorney General v. Sidley Memorial Hospital*, the Columbia Supreme Court found it appropriate to appear a monitor to oversee then defendant's day-to-day operations where a previous director and officer had received only cursory supervision from the board and, as a result, had engaged in numerous self-dealing transactions. Similarly, here, SIA's board appears to have only cursorily supervised the actions of Ellis and Zackler, who have engaged in self-dealing through KUK and the improper reimbursements. The court, here, would likely find a monitor similarly appropriate.

5.   Board Member Cruise

Remedies and Statutes

As discussed above, directors violate their fiduciary duties by engaging in self-interested transactions and in failing to act as a reasonably prudent person in their dealings with the corporation. The AG has broad equitable powers to ensure a charitable corporation's compliance with its trust. Nonprofit Corporation Law Section 5250. The AG has a "complete range of equitable remedies" at her disposal, and these include "injunctions to prevent and correct breach of fiduciary obligations arising from a trust." *Orange County Charitable Services*.

With respect to the board members' cruise, the AG might seek an accounting to determine whether the board members involved on the cruise actually engaged in long-range planning, might enjoin further expenditures of this sort, and might appoint a monitor to oversee operations and ensure that officers and directors no longer engage in self-dealing transactions. Nonprofit Corporation Law Section 6511(c).

Facts Supporting Remedies

Barber indicates that Ellis, Zackler, and Wanderly embarked on a 10-day cruise along with their spouses. Although it was described as a long-range planning meeting, the agenda only prescribed one hour of planning per day. In addition, the trip was booked through Wanderly Travel Service, owned by Melanie Wanderly, a member of the Board and one of the individuals invited on the cruise. The cruise was not inexpensive -- the payment to Wanderly was a total of $70,000 for ten days.

The AG would likely be able to demonstrate that this was a self-interested transaction that benefitted Wanderly. In addition, in the absence of any proof that there was a valid corporate purpose for the trip, the AG might be able to demonstrate that the funds were improperly diverted from the trust purpose. Indeed, the fact that Zackler described these as legitimate travel expenses to the board suggests some wrongdoing or at least extremely poor management. The court is likely to find that the appointment of a monitor is appropriate, as discussed above, to ensure that further self-interested transactions do not occur. In addition, AG might be successful in seeking to enjoin any future self-interested transactions, whether ratified by the board or not, due to the rampant misuse of SIA funds by directors and officers in the past.

Whether AG Could Successfully Seek Dissolution or a Receivership

The AG can seek to dissolve a charitable corporation on any of the three following grounds: (1) the corporation has seriously offended any of the statutes regulating corporations or charitable organizations; (2) the corporation has fraudulently abused or usurped corporate powers; or (3) the corporation has violated any provision of law by any act or default which under the law is ground for forfeiture of corporate existence. Nonprofit Corporation Law Section 6511(a).

Prior to seeking the dissolution of a charitable corporation, the AG must give 30-days prior notice of the act done or omitted to be done and the corporation must have failed to institute proceedings to correct the error within 30 days or failed after that to take the required corrective action. Nonprofit Corporation Law Section 6511(b).

The court may order dissolution if it deems dissolution "just and expedient." Nonprofit Corporation Law Section 6511(c). The court may also place the corporation under receivership to wind up the affairs of the corporation or order the board to wind up the corporation under court supervision. *Id.*

The decision whether to dissolve a charitable corporation is within the discretion of the trial court. *Attorney General v. Sidley Memorial Hospital* (Col. Supreme Ct. 1994) (citing *Attorney General v. The Children's Trust* (Col. Supreme Ct. 1971).

In determining whether dissolution is appropriate, a court should consider that the purpose of equity "is not to punish, but merely to take such action as may be necessary to prevent the recurrence of improper conduct." *Sidley Memorial Hospital*. The court can consider whether "voluntary action has been taken in good faith to minimize such conduct." *Id*.

Here, the court is likely to find that SIA has seriously offended a number of statutes regulating charitable organizations. It has failed to make required accountings under Uniform Act Section 125, its officers and directors have engaged in numerous self-dealing transactions under Nonprofit Corporation Law Section 5233, it has failed to comply with its trusts or departed from its purposes under Nonprofit Corporation Law Section 5250 by failing to hold and cancelling seminars, and it has harmed members of the public by failing to refund money as requested. The court might well find that grounds would exist for dissolution and receivership.

However, the court is not likely to dissolve SIA at this stage because it would not be just or expedient. The court likely will compare SIA's situation to the case in *Sidley Memorial Hospital*. In that case, two directors who were also officers took complete control of the management of the hospital and conspired to enrich themselves by favoring financial institutions with which they were affiliated. The rest of the board essentially abdicated its supervisory role. However, the Columbia Supreme Court found that dissolution was inappropriate in light of two factors. First, the practices identified by the AG were corrected and the directors involved in the wrongdoing had died. Second, there was no indication that any of the other directors were involved in fraudulent practices or profited personally from the failure of supervision; in fact, the charity was overall running well.

Similarly, here, the two individuals chiefly involve in the wrongdoing are either dead (Ellis) or stepping down (Zackler). In addition, the only other board member who appears to have profited from the failure of supervision, Wanderly, also is leaving the board. Two new board members have been nominated and new officers and a committee chair will be selected. In addition, a new Executive Director has been appointed who appears committed to changing the way SIA is operated. Finally, Barber reports that, like the defendant in *Sidley Memorial Hospital*, SIA is financially healthy, with a healthy reserve and many sources of revenue. In order to avoid dissolution, Barber should take further steps to remediate the wrongs done by Ellis and Zackler.

SELECTED ANSWER 2

TO: Sonia Sanchez
FROM: Applicant
DATE: July 30, 2013
RE: Objective Memorandum- re SIA

Ms. Sanchez:

This memorandum explains the potential liability that Sensory Integration Alliance, Inc. (SIA) faces as a result of the facts referenced below. Per your request, this memorandum does not address any of the Attorney General's (AG) possible remedies against individual transgressors.

I. Relevant Acts

SIA is a non-profit corporation that fundraises directly without the assistance of commercial fundraisers. Recently, several acts, including canceled and unscheduled seminars; questionable payments to Klene Up Kroo (KUK) Janitorial Services; unfiled Form 990s; questionable expense account reimbursements to Vernon Ellis (VE); and a cruise taken by board members have been identified as potential issues by the new executive Director, Karen Barber (KB). In addressing SIA's potential liabilities, it is necessary to have a general understanding of the state organizations with oversight over non-profit corporations.

The primary responsibility for supervising charitable organizations and ensuring compliance resides in the Attorney General (AG). *Charitable Purposes Act Section (CPAS)* 127. The AG has broad powers, including the ability to implement a charitable trust. *Id.* The AG may refuse to register or may revoke or suspend the registration of a charitable corporation or trustee or commercial fundraiser whenever there is a finding that said organization has violated the provisions of the *CPA*. Additionally, the AG can take other equitable actions.

Additionally, the AG can bring an action against a corporation in the name of the people on the basis of its own information or a complaint filed by a private party to procure a judgment dissolving the corporation and annulling, vacating or forfeiting its corporate existence. *CCCS* 6511.

Here, a complaint was submitted regarding SIA's failure to reimburse a client for a canceled seminar, providing the basis for the AG to potentially move forward. To do so, the AG must show that the corporation has seriously violated statutes regulating corporations or charitable organizations; the corporation has fraudulently abused or usurped corporate privileges or powers; or the corporation has violated a law by act or omission which is ground for forfeiture. *Id.*

Despite these potential remedies against SIA, if a problem can be corrected with an amendment to the articles or by other corporate action, no suit will be maintained unless the AG has given notice to the corporation within 30 days prior to the suit; and the corporation has failed to institute proceedings to correct it within the 30 day period, or fails to duly and properly take such action. *Id* at (b). Here, SIA has received proper notice and has two weeks to respond to avoid further investigation and action by the AG.

A.   Canceled or Unscheduled Seminars

1.   *Remedies & Statute*

A corporation is subject at all times to examination by the AG to ascertain the condition of its affairs, including to determine if it has departed from the purposes for which it was formed. *CCCS* 5250. In the case of failing to perform its purposes, the AG can take action necessary against a corporation to obtain compliance. *Id.* Under statutory law, the court can order restitutionary and/or injunctive relief to compensate or protect members of the public who have been harmed by the corporation's violations. *CCCS* 6511(c). The court can also order dissolution and/or appoint a receiver for winding up. *Id.* Finally, under the *CPAS* 127, the AG has the power to institute charitable trusts, to refuse to register and/or may revoke or suspend the registration of a charitable corporation.

Under case law, a violating corporation may be subject to other potential remedies for the individual violations made by its directors in defrauding the public. General remedies for vindicating the public interest in charitable assets include injunctions to prevent and correct breach of fiduciary obligations arising from a trust. In *OCCS*, the court enjoined a commercial fundraiser from making various false or misleading representations to prospective donors, directed them to make specified affirmative representations to prospective donors, barred them from soliciting for organizations which had not authorized them to do so, imposed certain reporting duties, directed them to account for their fundraising activities up to the date of judgment, enjoined them from commercial fundraising until a complete accounting was given, and required them to register as commercial fundraisers. Additionally, the court imposed a charitable trust on monies recovered under the accounting provisions of the judgment.

Directors and officers are agents of a corporation, meaning that a corporation can be liable for their actions. *See generally Sidley Memorial Hospital (SMH)*. Under the *Columbia Corporations Code Section (CCCS)* 5231, a director has a duty of loyalty to act in good faith in the best interest of the corporation as an ordinarily prudent person in like circumstances would. In executing these duties, a director can rely on information and opinions provided by counsel, independent accountants and other persons believed to be reliable and competent in the matters presented; or on a committee which the director does not sit on, if she relies in good faith and after reasonable inquiry. *CCCS* 5231(b).

2.   Likelihood of Remedy Being Imposed

Here, Vernon Ellis (VE) was the former executive director for SIA. Additionally, Alan Zackler (AZ) was a member of SIA's board and the Chair of the Budget and Finance Committee. Therefore, as a general matter both of them are agents for SIA and their actions can make SIA liable for damages, injunction, and potentially dissolution. *See OCCS & SMH*.

For the course of three years, VE was organizing and in some cases fraudulently purporting to organize seminars to fulfill the charitable purposes of SIA. The complaint initiating the AG's potential investigation into SIA was triggered by SIA's failure to report such an action. Recently KB discovered that VE had been writing reimbursement checks and depositing them into a personal account in Balfour Bank, a bank not used by SIA. VE's taking of $18,000 in refund checks over the course of three years violates his duty of loyalty to the corporation because an ordinarily prudent person would not steal from the corporation or from those attempting to participate in its seminars. Additionally, AZ, being aware of this, repeatedly hid these issues from the Board during their quarterly meetings in 2010, 2011, and 2012, violating his duty of loyalty. Thus, both VE and AZ have violated their duty of loyalty under the statute and potentially opened the rest of the board and SIA up to liability.

However, other directors and therefore the company are permitted to rely on the representations made by counsel, independent Accountants, or other persons competent. *CCCS* 5231(b). Additionally, directors are allowed to rely on a committee as long as the Board acts in good faith after reasonable inquiry when the circumstances warrant it. *Id.*

Here, as a defense, the Board and therefore the company can assert that they made reasonable inquiry into potential problems in financial reports. In 2011, Directors Garcia and Dunne questioned certain expenditures. Upon this questioning, AZ responded that he had reviewed each expenditure and that each was bona fide. In 2012, Director Dunne led a discussion about a concern of an apparent increase in staff travel reimbursements. AZ, as chair of the budget committee, explained the legitimacy of the expenses associated with this increase. Finally, in 2013, several directors expressed serious concern over the fact that the annual budget had not been prepared and over the Form 990s being filed, and again AZ assured them all was taken care of. While it is possible that a court would find these inquiries insufficient, at least those made after two years of concerns in 2013, they would likely hold up in protecting the corporation from liability on the failure of these directors. Therefore, it is unlikely that SIA could be held liable for the failure of these directors. However, SIA can still be held liable for the violation of statutes and abuse of corporate powers committed by VE and AZ.

Based on the potential remedies available to the AG and the specific harm caused by VE and AZ related to the embezzlement of charitable funds, SIA will likely face multiple remedies. These remedies will likely include restitutionary damages to those that paid for the seminars and were not reimbursed, possibly in the form of a constructive trust, and a potential injunction from engaging in charitable solicitations until a full accounting of these reimbursements has been assured to the AG. Additionally, SIA faces a potential suspension or indefinite revocation of their registration as a charitable corporation.

B.   Payments for Klene Up Kroo Janitorial Services

1.   *Remedies & Statute*
Please see the remedies listed in A(1) above.

2.   *Likelihood of Remedy Being Imposed*
Here, VE and AZ were involved in breaching their duty of loyalty owed to the corporation. However, this action was not fraud against the public, but fraud against the company in the multiple misrepresentations made during the 2011-2013 quarterly meetings. A self-dealing transaction is one where one or more of the directors have a material financial interest, and where the transaction was: 1) entered into by the corporation for its own benefit; 2) the transaction was fair and reasonable; or 3) pre-transaction, the Board approved it in good faith by a majority of the directors in the office with knowledge of the material facts. *CCCS* 5233(a), (d).

Here, bank records supported a finding that VE wrote checks to a company, KUK, for janitorial services totaling $22,000. The facts show that while the checks were made out to Howard Klene, withdrawals from his account were then deposited into VE's personal account in Arden Bank. Disbursements from this account were regularly made to VE and AZ, showing again that they breached their fiduciary duties owed to the corporation by self-dealing. Records show that each of them absconded with $8,000, money SIA might be able to recover later. Because there is no indication that SIA received the benefit of said janitorial services or that there was any board approval, VE and AZ will remain in violation of their fiduciary duties.

There is an exception to self-dealing. It will not apply when the transaction is a part of a public charitable program of the corporation if it is approved or authorized in good faith without unjustified favoritism, and if it results in the benefit of one or more directors or their families because they are in the class of persons to be benefited by the public or charitable program. *CCCS 5223*(b). Because there is no indication that janitorial services are relevant to SIA's purposes of helping those with sensory disabilities, this exception does not apply. Therefore, VE and AZ remain liable for their breaches of fiduciary duties.

While these violations did not harm the public directly, SIA will still be liable for VE and AZ's violation of statute and abuse of corporate power. Because there was no harm to the public, it is unlikely that restitutionary or other damages will be implemented by the AG. However, as will be explained below, such actions may lead to other injunctive relief, or dissolution. Other injunctive relief might include an injunction from raising charitable funds until there is evidence that such fiduciary problems no longer pose a risk. *See SMH*.

C.   Unfiled Form 990s

1.   Remedies & Statute

Public benefit corporations and commercial fundraisers must file annual reports, including Form 990, an informational tax return filed with the IRS annually. *Charitable Purposes Act Section (CPAS)* 125(a); *OC Charitable Services (OCCS)* (1998). This form must be filed no later than four months and fifteen days after the close of the first fiscal year upon registration. *Id.* at (b). Said corporations may be fined $25 for each month or part month it fails to file its first and subsequent 990 forms. *Id.* at (c). The contents include information about sources and amounts of income, salaries for key employees, a list of board members and their compensation, and the top five consultant fees. *Id.*

2. *Likelihood of Remedy Being Imposed*

Here, SIA faces liability for VE's failure to file Form 990 for the years of 2010, 2011, and 2012. This violation is straightforward in terms of SIA's liability. At a minimum, SIA will be liable for a $25/month fee for the three years it has failed to file the form. The IRS has contacted SIA putting them on notice that they had not received the required forms, eliminating any likelihood of reasonable excuse. Additionally, their other concerns include the inaccuracy contained in the statements. If SIA were to submit inaccurate statements, it would be committing fraud and exposing itself to more severe actions by the AG. *See OCCS.* Potential remedies for filing false reports would be an injunction from fundraising for charitable purposes until there was a correct accounting. *Id.* Therefore, SIA should seek to find the correct information to report to the IRS.

Finally, as stated above, this failure may be considered in the overall determination of whether the AG will seek to take injunctive action or be justified in seeking a dissolution of SIA. However, alone it will not merit an injunction.

D. Expense Account Reimbursements to Vernon Ellis

1. *Remedies & Statute*

Please see the remedies listed in A(1) above.

2. *Likelihood of Remedy Being Imposed*

Here, again VE and AZ engaged in violations of their fiduciary duties by breaching their duty of loyalty to SIA by self-dealing. Evidence demonstrates that VE used SIA funds for non-charitable purposes, including personal dinner parties, cocktails, and other things. Particularly egregious was the fact that VE would use the company credit card to pay for these things and then seek personal reimbursement (double-dipping).

While these breaches of fiduciary duties will not expose SIA to restitutionary or other damages, they will likely be a factor in determining whether the AG will bring an injunction of some kind or seek dissolution of SIA.

E.   Cruise taken By Board Members

1.   Remedies & Statute
Please see the remedies listed in A(1) above.

2.   Likelihood of Remedy Being Imposed

In this instance, VE, AZ, Melanie Wanderly (MW), and their spouses appeared to have possibly used corporate funds to take a $70,000 ten-day cruise. Because there is no evidence that any actual business discussions or purposes took place on that trip, it is likely another breach of fiduciary duty by all three. This time, another member of the Board, MW, is involved. All three of these directors breached their duty of loyalty by using corporate funds for personal recreation absent a reasonable business purpose, failing to act as a reasonably prudent director would. Additionally, the fact that the check was made to Wanderly Travel Service suggests self-dealing on the part of MW. Therefore, all three of these directors breached these duties, making SIA potentially liable for the abuse of corporate powers.

Again, these breaches will not likely result in any kind of restitutionary or other damages, but will be relevant in the determination of an injunction or the potential forced dissolution of SIA.

II.   Attorney General's (AG) Likelihood of Obtaining A Receivership or Dissolution of SIA

As stated above, a corporation is subject at all times to examination by the AG to ascertain the condition of its affairs, including to determine if it has departed from the purposes for which it was formed. *CCCS* 5250. In the case of failing to perform its purposes, the AG can take action necessary against a corporation to obtain compliance. *Id.* Under statutory law, the court can order restitutionary and/or injunctive relief to compensate or protect members of the public who have been harmed by the corporation's violations. *CCCS* 6511(c). The court can also order dissolution and/or appoint a receiver for winding up. *Id.*

According to the court in *Sidley Memorial Hospital (SMH)*, the function of equity is not to punish but merely to take such action as may be necessary to prevent the recurrence of improper conduct. (1994). A court will consider voluntary action taken in good faith to minimize such recurrences. *Id.* In *SMH*, the court found that forcing a dissolution was too harsh where there was a severe and continuous breach of fiduciary duties by two controlling officers. *Id.* Instead, the court appointed a monitor to manage the company's day-to-day operations until the court determined such supervision was no longer necessary. *Id.*

Here, the situation involving VE and AZ, and to a lesser extent, MW, is similar to *SMH*. In both situations there were rogue directors taking actions in breach of their fiduciary duties, and in some cases, deceiving and defrauding the public. The directors in *SMH* breached their fiduciary duties and violated Columbia statutes in the *CCC* and *CPA*. VE, and AZ to the extent that he covered up VE's violations of the *CPA*, also violated these acts. Despite all of this the court decided not to dissolve the corporation at issue in *SMH*. The court's reasons were several, including the fact that the directors creating the problems and violating the laws were no longer a part of the organization. Further, the new directors were making good faith efforts to account for the errors of their predecessors. *SMH*. In other words, voluntary action was taken in good faith to remedy and prevent the recurrence of similar improper conduct. *Id.* Finally, there was no indication that other directors were participating in the fraudulent conduct.

Based off the reasoning in *SMH*, it is unlikely that a court would uphold a remedy seeking dissolution and receivership by the AG because SIA has acted similar to *SMH*. Specifically, VE, AZ, and MW are no longer members of the board, VE having died and AZ and MW having finished their terms. Additionally, the new directors, including KB are making good faith efforts to remedy the previous violations and get SIA back on track. That said, while it is unlikely for a dissolution to be granted, SIA does face the potential that the court will appoint a monitor to manage its day-to-day actions.

III.   Conclusion

In conclusion, SIA may be liable for restitutionary damages, likely in the form of a charitable trust, to the members of the public that were defrauded by VE for his cancellation of seminars. Additionally, SIA will likely be subject to some kind of injunction in fundraising for VE's violations of their charitable purpose. While it is possible for the AG to seek a suspension or revocation of SIA's registration as a charitable corporation, it is unlikely given the precedent in *OCCS*, where the corporate actions were far more egregious and did not result in such a suspension or revocation. Finally, the AG will likely not be successful in bringing an action for dissolution, but the court may appoint a monitor.

If you have any follow-up questions or other concerns regarding this matter, please let me know how I can be of assistance.

Sincerely,
The Applicant

July 2013

California
Bar
Examination

Performance Test B
INSTRUCTIONS AND FILE

PEOPLE v. DRAPER

Instructions . . . .

FILE

Memorandum from Milo Ward to Applicant . . . .

Transcript of Hearing . . . .

PEOPLE v. DRAPER

INSTRUCTIONS

1. This performance test is designed to evaluate your ability to handle a select number of legal authorities in the context of a factual problem involving a client.

2. The problem is set in the fictional State of Columbia, one of the United States.

3. You will have two sets of materials with which to work: a File and a Library.

4. The File contains factual materials about your case. The first document is a memorandum containing the instructions for the tasks you are to complete.

5. The Library contains the legal authorities needed to complete the tasks. The case reports may be real, modified, or written solely for the purpose of this performance test. If the cases appear familiar to you, do not assume that they are precisely the same as you have read before. Read each thoroughly, as if it were new to you. You should assume that cases were decided in the jurisdictions and on the dates shown. In citing cases from the Library, you may use abbreviations and omit page citations.

6. You should concentrate on the materials provided, but you should also bring to bear on the problem your general knowledge of the law. What you have learned in law school and elsewhere provides the general background for analyzing the problem; the File and Library provide the specific materials with which you must work.

7. Although there are no restrictions on how you apportion your time, you should probably allocate at least 90 minutes to reading and organizing before you begin preparing your response.

8. Your response will be graded on its compliance with instructions and on its content, thoroughness, and organization.

MEMORANDUM

TO: Applicant

FROM: Deputy District Attorney Milo Ward

DATE: August 1, 2013

RE: People v. Draper

Our office is prosecuting a domestic battery case against Horace Draper. Mr. Draper allegedly struck his wife, Sarah Morris, causing serious injuries. While Ms. Morris's initial statement to the 911 Dispatcher supported the charge of battery of a spouse, Ms. Morris has since changed her story, and now states that her injuries were accidental.

As you know, our office will continue with prosecutions even when the complaining witness declines to cooperate when we believe there is sufficient evidence. Thus, we are proceeding to trial on this case. We intend to call a domestic violence expert, Professor Pamela Simoni, to explain that it is typical in battering situations for women to recant. The defense requested an evidentiary hearing under Evidence Code section 402. We just completed that hearing where we called Professor Simoni as a witness to preview her testimony at trial. The judge wants briefing on the admissibility of Professor Simoni's testimony.

Please draft a memo in which you analyze which portions of Professor Simoni's testimony are admissible, and which portions are not. I will use the memo to help me draft the post-hearing brief requested by the judge.

Do not write a separate Statement of Facts, but incorporate the facts into your analysis where appropriate.

TRANSCRIPT OF HEARING

JUDGE LELAND PARKER (JUDGE): We're back in session in the matter of People v. Draper. Counsel, I'd like the record to reflect that we are conducting this hearing outside the presence of the jury. In its pretrial disclosures, the People indicated that they would be calling a domestic violence expert witness at trial. The defense has objected on several grounds, and I am holding this evidentiary hearing to be followed by submission of simultaneous briefs by the People and by the defense. I will issue my ruling in time for us to proceed with trial on Monday. Counsel, please state your appearances.

AMY FORTNER (DA): Amy Fortner, Deputy District Attorney, for the People, Your Honor.

NAOMI REVELLE (PD): Naomi Revelle, Your Honor, Deputy Public Defender, representing the defendant, Horace Draper.

JUDGE: Ms. Fortner, please proceed.

DA: Thank you, Your Honor. The People would like to play a 911 tape recorded at about 7:00 a.m. on June 5, 2012.

PD: The Defense stipulates that this is an authentic recording and that the voice of the caller is that of Sarah Morris, the Defendant's wife.

JUDGE: Please play the tape.

[Clerk plays the tape.]

> **Dispatcher:** This is 911. How can I help you?
>
> **Caller:** My husband hit me. I'm bleeding. I can't breathe.
>
> **Dispatcher:** Ma'am, try to calm down. Where are you bleeding?
>
> **Caller:** My mouth.
>
> **Dispatcher:** Do you feel faint?
>
> **Caller:** No, it just hurts and there's blood everywhere.
>
> **Dispatcher:** Is there a way you can get to the hospital?
>
> **Caller:** No, I can't. My husband took my car keys.
>
> **Dispatcher:** Ma'am, what's your name?
>
> **Caller:** Sarah Morris.

Dispatcher: Who hurt you?

Caller: My husband.

Dispatcher: What's his name?

Caller: Horace Draper.

Dispatcher: Is he still there?

Caller: No, he must have taken my car.

Dispatcher: Do you have any idea where he went?

Caller: No, I don't.

Dispatcher: Sarah, are you calling from 765 Fordham Lane?

Caller: Yes, I am.

Dispatcher: The police are on their way. Do you need an ambulance?

Caller: No, I think it's just my mouth. I'm going to see if someone can take me to the dentist.

Dispatcher: Sarah, please wait until the police arrive, okay?

Caller: Okay.

Dispatcher: Stay on the line with me until they arrive, okay?

Caller: Okay.

[End of tape.]

DA: The People call Paul Morris.

[The witness is sworn.]

DA: Mr. Morris, are you related to the Defendant, Horace Draper?

PAUL MORRIS (W-1): Yes, he's my brother-in-law. He's married to my sister, Sarah Morris.

DA: On June 5, 2012, did you go to your sister and brother-in-law's house at 765 Fordham Lane?

W-1: Yes, I did.

DA: What happened when you got there?

W-1: As I approached the house, Horace Draper came running out.

DA: What happened next?

W-1: He said that there had been an accident.

DA: Did he say anything else?

W-1: He said that he and Sarah were arguing because he had taken $120 from her purse to pay the gardener. He said that Sarah then swung her purse at him, and when he tried to calm her down, she accidentally got hit in the mouth. I asked Horace if Sarah was all right and he said that he didn't know.

DA: Then what?

W-1: Horace said that all she did after that was glare at him and run into the bathroom. He said that she was probably okay. Before I could say anything else, Horace ran off to Sarah's car and drove away.

DA: What did you do then?

W-1: I ran inside and up to Sarah's room. I heard her in the bathroom and ran to the door. She was there with a towel trying to stop the bleeding from her mouth and face.

DA: What did you see?

W-1: Sarah had a bloody mouth and a large bruise on her neck and shoulder area. She put up her hand and said, "I've already called 911; the police are coming."

DA: Then what?

W-1: We waited for the police. They were there at the house for about half an hour. After they left, Sarah asked me to take her to the dentist.

DA: And is that what you did?

W-1: Yes, we went there in my car and I was there with her for five hours.

DA: Mr. Morris, do you know Horace Draper well?

W-1: Yes, I live in the neighborhood and go over there a lot -- at least once a week.

DA: Had Horace and your sister's financial situation changed in the six months before this incident?

W-1: Yes, Horace had lost his job and hadn't been able to find a new one.

DA: What about Sarah?

W-1: She had just gotten a promotion to office manager where she works.

DA: How did Horace feel about this?

W-1: He was a lot moodier and got upset a lot more after he lost his job. He said he wanted Sarah to quit her job. He also said that he was making her give him all her paychecks because he couldn't trust her any more.

DA: Have you talked to your sister about this?

W-1: Yes.

DA: When's the last time?

W-1: About a month before this happened. She said she was feeling horrible, anxious and depressed. She said she felt like she couldn't do anything right.

DA: I have nothing further for Mr. Morris, Your Honor.

JUDGE: Do you have any questions?

PD: We have no questions.

JUDGE: Call your next witness.

DA: The People call Dr. Cathy Tucker.

[The witness is sworn.]

DA: Dr. Tucker, do you know Sarah Morris?

CATHY TUCKER (W-2): Yes, I do.

DA: How do you know her?

W-2: She is a patient of mine in my dental practice.

DA: When did you last see her?

W-2: Ms. Morris came into my office on June 5, 2012 at around 10:00 a.m. She had a pretty badly split lip, a significantly swollen mouth, extensive bleeding, and a loose tooth. I gave her emergency treatment, consisting of an exam, x-rays, a tooth extraction, a root canal, and insertion of a stay plate. The treatment took four and one-half hours.

DA: Dr. Tucker, do you have experience with these kinds of injuries?

W-2: Yes, I have observed and treated about 200 impact injuries. I believe that Ms. Morris's injuries were caused by a high-impact blow, rather than a low-impact blow.

DA: We have nothing further for Dr. Tucker.

JUDGE: Any questions for this witness, Ms. Revelle?

PD: No, Your Honor.

JUDGE: Call your next witness.

DA: The People call Professor Pamela Simoni.

[The witness is sworn.]

DA: Your Honor, we are calling Professor Simoni to testify on the eight following subjects: (1) the typical profile of a batterer; (2) patterns of behavior of batterers and battering victims; (3) the cycle of violence; (4) recantation; (5) behavior right after the abuse; (6) the so-called "window" and why it closes; (7) why victims return to the relationship; and, (8) the posing of a hypothetical. Professor Simoni, please tell the Court a little about your background.

PAMELA SIMONI (W-3): I am an attorney and a law professor. I have practiced in the area of domestic violence law for almost 30 years. Right out of law school I began a project at the Franklin County Legal Aid Society that trained advocates about how to work with victims of domestic violence. I also designed and conducted training programs for law enforcement agencies on the nature of domestic violence. After that, I worked for five years as the legal director for a program that was part of a larger domestic violence agency in Oakmont in Sanford County.

I have been teaching a Domestic Violence Seminar at the University of Columbia School of Law since 1990. I am the author of a textbook on the subject that is used in many undergraduate and law schools in the country.

I also served on the board of the Columbia Partnership to End Domestic Violence, where I helped draft and work toward the passage of legislation benefiting victims of domestic violence and their children. I currently consult and testify as an expert witness on domestic violence in criminal prosecution, defense, family law, asylum, and tort cases.

DA: Professor Simoni, how many times have you testified as an expert?

W-3: At least 60 times.

DA: Professor Simoni, have you ever met the defendant Horace Draper, or his spouse, Sarah Morris?

W-3: No, I have not.

DA: Approximately how many victims of domestic violence have you worked with?

W-3: About 1000, I would say.

DA: Of these 1000 domestic violence victims, how many have been women?

W-3: All but a handful.

DA: Professor Simoni, based on your extensive work with domestic violence victims and your familiarity with the literature, is it your opinion that there is a typical profile of a battering male?

W-3: There is no typical profile in terms of socioeconomic status or race of a male batterer. All classes and races are represented. I will say that there are commonly recurring characteristics of batterers. For instance, a typical male batterer, in the beginning of a relationship, will be charming, romantic and intense. He will also, however, be rigid in his views regarding how men and women should behave in a relationship. Men who batter are frequently jealous. In addition, 50 to 60 percent of cases involving a batterer involve the use of alcohol or drugs. The male batterer will make his partner dependent and attack her self-esteem.

DA: Your Honor, the People request that Professor Simoni be qualified as an expert in this case.

PD: We have no objection to Professor Simoni's qualifications and we agree that in appropriate cases the nature of domestic violence is the proper subject matter for expert testimony. We object to this testimony in this case, however. There is no evidence that Mr. Draper fits the male batterer profile or that Ms. Morris suffers from battered woman's syndrome. The evidence will show that this is the first injury that Ms. Morris has ever suffered during her marriage.

JUDGE: The witness is qualified as an expert. Counsel, your objections are preserved. I will rule on the admissibility of Professor Simoni's testimony after this hearing and after reading your briefs.

DA: Thank you, Your Honor. Professor Simoni, are there typical patterns of behavior exhibited by male batterers and female battering victims?

W-3: Yes. Typically, the woman begins to believe that she can't trust her friends; that her family interferes; that her male friends are only after sex; that she's fat, stupid, ugly, and incompetent; that she's crazy, hypersensitive, and hysterical all the time; that nobody would ever want her; and that she's really, really lucky to be in this relationship with this guy. The man will start to blame the woman for everything that goes on around him. He will use coercion, threats and intimidation to maintain control of his partner. A batterer will sometimes coerce the woman into sexual acts. He may force her to watch pornographic movies and ask her to engage in some of the activities portrayed in the films. If she does not wish to engage in the sexual activities, he will tell her that she is not normal sexually. A batterer will try to get his partner to do some things that sort of cross her own bottom line. And when he's able to do that, he's able to get her to feel guilty and ashamed about things that are going on in their relationship, things that she's uncomfortable with; then he begins to make threats.

DA: Professor Simoni, can you describe the cycle of violence in the context of domestic violence?

W-3: Yes, once a woman has committed to a relationship with a batterer, a cycle of violence begins. The batterer has an absolute need for power and control over his female partner. The relationship usually follows a three-phase cycle. The first and longest phase is referred to as the "tension-building period." The second phase involves actual physical violence. Finally, there is a "honeymoon" or "hooking back" phase.

DA: Can you describe the tension-building phase?

W-3: During the tension-building period, the batterer criticizes his partner. When she becomes upset, he says he was only joking and she is being hysterical. Although the relationship may appear to be going well, the man will start to emotionally abuse his partner by calling her names and insulting her. The batterer will then isolate the woman from her friends, co-workers, and family. Economic control is a common element in abusive relationships and it does not matter whether the man or woman is earning the greater amount of money. Not every one of these factors is present in every relationship. Each batterer tends to have a favorite tactic.

DA: Can you talk about your experiences with women who report a first incident of violence?

W-3: Yes, about 80 percent of the time a woman who has been "initially assaulted" by a boyfriend, husband or lover will recant, change or minimize her story. This recanting does not happen only after there has been a continuing pattern of abuse. In fact, depending on the severity of the incident, it is more likely to occur after a first incident. A woman will tend to minimize and deny the incident. The woman will engage in "self-blame" and sort of recharacterize the incident, especially if the relationship is going to continue. It's the most common reaction of anybody who's been victimized in an intimate relationship.

DA: Do you ever see instances when the first incidence of violence in an intimate relationship occurs years after the marriage began?

W-3: Yes, I am describing typical patterns, but every battering relationship is different. I would say that you describe an unusual, but not rare, situation.

DA: Can you explain a bit more about the typical behavior of the victim of the abuse right after the abuse occurs?

W-3: She begins to feel guilty and responsible. When a violent act takes place, she is usually terrified and shocked. The woman never expected this person that she loves -- this wonderful, romantic, charming guy she's in love with -- to physically hurt her. When the actual violent event occurs, the woman is able to feel and recall the details of the event. This short period is referred to as a "window." However, the window will stay open only if the woman leaves the relationship and has support in the outside community. If the woman has contact with the batterer, the window will close.

DA: Why does the window close?

W-3: The batterer will start a "honeymoon" period and will tell the woman he loves her, that the incident was an accident, and that he never meant to hurt her. The batterer will make the woman promise she will not talk to anyone about the incident, that she will not go to court, and that she will tell the police she lied about the violence.

DA: Are there other reasons why the window closes?

W-3: This window may close for financial reasons, because of the woman's lack of self-esteem, or because of her loneliness. The woman will lose sight of what actually happened and begin to believe the batterer's version of events. She may become angry with prosecutors, the judge, and everyone else in the courtroom. She begins to think of her attacker as the one who is misunderstood.

DA: Would you expand a bit on recantation among domestic violence victims?

W-3: Generally, when an abused woman discusses a battering event, she will tell a "different story" by recanting or minimizing the event. If a woman wishes the relationship with her batterer to continue, she will tell the police and the prosecutor that the violent incident never occurred. A woman will react in this manner more commonly after the first event because she really wants to believe that the person who committed the act of violence is not the man she is in love with.

DA: And do you find when these women are removed from contact with the abuser or the abuser's family, they tend to be honest about what's happened or are they still reluctant once they have been separated from that situation?

W-3: Much more likely to be honest.

DA: Now you're not saying every battered woman tells the truth all the time, are you?

W-3: No, of course not.

DA: In fact, don't they lie on occasion?

W-3: Yes, they do.

DA: And you find, based on the statements that you just made, that they're more likely to be honest within 24 to 48 hours after the incident?

W-3: Yes.

DA: Do battered women, in your experience, go back to their abusers?

W-3: Yes, they do.

DA: Why do they go back, based on your training and experience?

W-3: Because they love them; they're not sure how they can survive on their own; pressure from family and friends; or because their children want to be with their father.

DA: I'd like to pose a hypothetical question to you, Professor. If a single incidence of violence in an intimate relationship is preceded by the loss of a job by the husband three months before the violence and is accompanied by a job promotion to the wife, increased moodiness in the husband, and demands by the husband that the wife quit her job and turn over her paychecks to him, are these occurrences typical of the "tension-building" stage of the cycle of violence?

W-3: Yes, I would say so. I would also say that these behaviors are consistent with the "power and control wheel" -- a model developed to describe typical kinds of behaviors or characteristics that are present in abusive relationships. At the center of the wheel are the words "power and control." The battering partner's goal is to exert control over the victim partner. To do so, he or she may use a variety of methods, including demeaning and humiliating the other partner, monitoring and controlling their access to other people, minimizing the seriousness of the abuse, and denying the other partner access to money.

DA: Thank you, Professor Simoni. Your Honor, I have nothing further.

JUDGE: Thank you, Professor. You are excused. Counsel, I would like both of you to submit briefs, due tomorrow at noon. I will rule on both the admissibility of Professor Simoni's testimony, as well as any limits on the scope of that testimony if I permit it. We are now in recess.

July 2013

California
Bar
Examination

Performance Test B
LIBRARY

PEOPLE v. DRAPER

LIBRARY

Selected Provisions of the Columbia Evidence Code . . . .

People v. Gould
Columbia Court of Appeal (2002) . . . .

People v. Bowen
Columbia Court of Appeal (2004) . . . .

People v. Slater
Columbia Court of Appeal (2008) . . . .

Selected Provisions of the Columbia Evidence Code

Section 352.

The court in its discretion may exclude evidence if its probative value is substantially outweighed by the probability that its admission will (a) necessitate undue consumption of time or (b) create substantial danger of undue prejudice, of confusing the issues, or of misleading the jury.

Section 402.

(a)   When the existence of a preliminary fact is disputed, its existence or nonexistence shall be determined as provided in this article.

(b)   The court may hear and determine the question of the admissibility of evidence out of the presence or hearing of the jury; but in a criminal action, the court shall hear and determine the question of the admissibility of a confession or admission of the defendant out of the presence and hearing of the jury if any party so requests.

Section 801.

If a witness is testifying as an expert, his testimony in the form of an opinion is limited to such an opinion as is:

(a)   Related to a subject that is sufficiently beyond common experience that the opinion of an expert would assist the trier of fact; and

(b)   Based on matter (including his special knowledge, skill, experience, training, and education) perceived by or personally known to the witness or made known to him at or before the hearing, whether or not admissible, that is of a type that reasonably may be relied upon by an expert in forming an opinion upon the subject to which his testimony relates, unless an expert is precluded by law from using such matter as a basis for his opinion.

People v. Gould

Columbia Court of Appeal (2002)

In this case, we decide expert testimony regarding battered woman's syndrome is not relevant unless there is sufficient factual evidence that the victim is a battered woman.

A jury found Daniel R. Gould (Gould) guilty of assault against his wife, Mary Dean (Dean), under circumstances involving domestic violence.

Gould contends the trial court erred when it allowed the prosecutor to present expert testimony regarding battered woman's syndrome. He argues this expert testimony was irrelevant because no evidence showed the victim in this case was suffering from battered woman's syndrome. He further asserts the evidence was highly prejudicial and its admission requires reversal of his convictions. We agree and reverse the judgment.

Prior to trial, the prosecutor indicated she intended to present expert testimony regarding battered woman's syndrome. The expert, Gail Peale (Peale), is the director of a domestic abuse center. The prosecutor asserted Peale's testimony was necessary to show "why women who have been assaulted by their husbands or boyfriends later recant, minimize, suffer memory lapses due to post-traumatic stress, and decline to 'prosecute' their assailants, especially after the first incident of violence."

Outside the presence of the jury the court conducted an evidentiary hearing pursuant to Evidence Code section 402. After the hearing, the trial court indicated it would allow the testimony on a limited basis. The court stated, "I want to limit the issues. This is an expert on domestic violence. The testimony should be limited to how victims of domestic violence minimize the violence, recant and decline to prosecute. I want you to avoid the use of the words 'battered woman's syndrome,' because I don't think there's been any evidence that she had any previous battering." The court concluded, "This witness is admitted as an expert on people who cohabitate as husband and wife, and to explain what they do, whether they've ever been battered before or not."

Peale testified she had never met Dean or Gould. Peale gave a lengthy explanation of the typical "male batterer." She also testified about the "three phases of domestic violence."

Gould contends that the expert's testimony regarding battered woman's syndrome was irrelevant because there was no evidence Dean had suffered ongoing abuse or battering. He argues the evidence was highly prejudicial under Evidence Code section 352, and its admission requires reversal of his convictions. The trial court stated the evidence would not be based on a finding that this was a battered woman but would be admitted only to assist the jury to understand that in a cohabitation situation, the women generally decline to prosecute, especially when they're going to go back to the man. The People contend the expert's testimony was relevant and properly admitted for a limited purpose. They further assert that if any error occurred, it was harmless.

DISCUSSION

1. Since There Was No Evidence Dean Had Suffered Ongoing Abuse of Battering, Peale's Testimony Was Irrelevant.

Whether expert testimony regarding battered woman's syndrome is admissible in a particular case initially depends on whether that evidence is relevant. In making a determination of relevancy, the court must first decide whether the evidence in the particular case supports a contention that the petitioner suffered ongoing abuse or battering. Expert testimony on battered woman's syndrome is irrelevant unless there is a sufficient factual basis for the fact that petitioner experienced ongoing abuse or battering.

Unlike the situation where there are multiple incidents of physical violence, or acts of psychological or emotional abuse, in the present case there is no evidence, with the exception of the present incident, to indicate Dean is in a battering relationship. There was no evidence that Gould had previously battered Dean or that they were engaged in an ongoing abusive relationship.

The People assert it was not necessary to show Dean had previously been abused by Gould. They refer to Peale's testimony that it is especially likely a woman will recant, minimize or completely deny the first violent incident.

That may be true, but the mere fact that Dean might have minimized or denied a single instance of violence or abuse does not mean she suffers from battered woman's syndrome. Battered woman's syndrome is a series of characteristics which appear in women who have been abused physically and psychologically over a period of time. A single violent incident, without evidence of other physical or psychological abuse, is not sufficient to establish that a woman suffers from battered woman's syndrome.

Here, other than evidence of the present incident, there is no evidence indicating that Gould abused or behaved violently toward Dean. There is no evidence that Gould fit the profile of a batterer, or that Dean and Gould were engaged in a "battering" relationship. On this record, Peale's testimony regarding battered woman's syndrome was irrelevant.

The People must present proper foundational evidence before they may use expert testimony regarding battered woman's syndrome to explain why a woman may recant, minimize or completely deny a violent incident. In the present case, Peale's testimony regarding battered woman's syndrome was irrelevant and the trial court erred in admitting it.

2.   **Admission of the Expert's Testimony Was Prejudicial.**

We cannot ignore Peale's powerful testimony and its likely effect on the jury. Peale's testimony was authoritative. She was presented as a highly qualified expert. Her testimony was lengthy and dramatic. She explained in detail the several cycles of a typical battering relationship. She extensively described the male batterer, explaining how he first charms, then demeans and insults his partner. Peale described a battering man as someone who both psychologically and physically brutalizes a woman to satisfy his need for power and control. She compared the relationship between a battering man and a battered woman to a condition called the "Stockholm Syndrome" which occurs when a hostage begins to view her "attacker" as "the good guy." Peale testified a batterer is often referred to as a "Dr. Jekyll and Mr. Hyde."

Both the trial court and the prosecutor emphasized Peale's inflammatory testimony. Our review of the whole record indicates it is reasonably probable that the jury would have reached a result more favorable to Gould had the court excluded Peale's testimony.

The judgment is reversed.

People v. Bowen

Columbia Court of Appeal (2004)

At defendant Michael Bowen's trial on charges relating to domestic violence, the prosecution offered testimony from an expert witness to explain that domestic violence victims often later deny or minimize the assailant's conduct. Defendant objected. He contended such testimony did not fall within the scope of Evidence Code section 801, which authorizes expert testimony. He argued the prosecution had failed to show that the victim here was a battered woman because it offered no proof that defendant had abused her on more than one occasion. The trial court overruled the objection and admitted the evidence. Defendant was convicted and appealed.

We conclude that in this case the evidence was admissible under Evidence Code section 801, because it would assist the trier of fact in evaluating the credibility of the victim's trial testimony and earlier statements to the police, by providing relevant information about the tendency of victims of domestic violence later to recant or minimize their description of that violence.

Defendant and Kimberly Laforge (Laforge), the victim, had been dating on and off for about 11 years. On April 17, 2001, they were living together in an apartment with Laforge's four children and Carrie Miller (Miller), a woman who took care of the children when Laforge worked.

Laforge rented the apartment from Leland Jones (Jones), Defendant's cousin. At 2 a.m. on April 17, Jones came to the apartment to demand payment of back rent. When Laforge refused because Jones had not fixed the water system, Jones told Laforge to vacate the apartment. After Jones left, Laforge and Defendant began arguing. Laforge was upset because she thought Defendant should have taken her side in the argument with Jones.

Shortly thereafter, Deputy Sheriff James Wheeler responded to a telephone call from Laforge and found her with Carrie Miller in a parked car near the apartment. Laforge told Deputy Wheeler she had been assaulted. She said she tried to leave the apartment after an argument with Defendant but he put his arm around her neck and dragged her to the bedroom. Defendant then went to the living room and returned to the bedroom with a steak knife and a barbecue fork, telling Laforge he would kill her if she left. She was afraid. When she said she wanted to leave, Defendant replied, "I don't want you having my baby," and punched her in the stomach. Miller told Deputy Wheeler that Defendant had threatened to kill both her and Laforge if they left. He also threatened to have some women come over to beat up Miller and Laforge. Deputy Wheeler arrested Defendant and found the steak knife where Laforge said it was.

Laforge's trial testimony differed from what she had told Deputy Wheeler earlier. At trial she said that when she started to leave the apartment, Defendant took hold of her arm, not her neck, and pulled her back to the bedroom. She lay down for a while, then when she got up to leave again he slapped her in the stomach. Defendant had never struck her before. She lay down again for a few minutes, then she woke Miller up, went with Miller and the children to the car, drove a short distance, and called the police. Laforge said that Defendant never threatened her.

Laforge testified that when she went into the apartment with the police, the officers said they did not have "enough to go on." Laforge then picked up the knife and fork and said Defendant had "poked" them at her. Laforge said she did this so Defendant would get arrested; in fact, he did not threaten her with the knife and fork. When asked whether Defendant was doing anything against her will, Laforge replied, "Not to the full extent, no."

Carrie Miller was not available to testify at the trial, so the prosecutor read to the jury Miller's testimony from the preliminary hearing. There Miller testified that she was asleep until Laforge woke her just before they left the apartment, so she did not know what happened between Laforge and Defendant. Laforge denied that Defendant had ever threatened her.

Jeri Parker (Parker), Program Manager of the Arnett Valley Domestic Violence Council, testified as an expert witness for the prosecution. Before permitting the jury to consider Parker's testimony, the trial court instructed: "This evidence is not going to be received and must not be considered by you to prove the occurrence of the act or acts of abuse which form the basis of the crimes charged." Parker testified: Domestic violence victims, after describing the violence to the police, often later repudiate their description. There is typically "anywhere between 24 and 48 hours where victims will be truthful about what occurred because they're still angry; they're still scared." But "after they have had time to think about it ... it is not uncommon for them to change their mind." About 80 to 85 percent of victims "actually recant at some point in the process." Some victims will say they lied to the police; almost all will attempt to minimize their experience.

Parker explained why victims of domestic violence may give conflicting statements: They may be financially dependent on the defendant. They may be pressured, or even threatened, by the defendant or other family members. They may still love the defendant and hope that things will get better.

Defendant objected to the admission of Parker's testimony.

The jury convicted Defendant on three counts: threatening to commit a crime that would result in death or great bodily injury against Laforge; false imprisonment by violence against Laforge; and misdemeanor battery against Laforge.

Evidence Code section 801, subdivision (a), permits the introduction of testimony by a qualified expert when that testimony may "assist the trier of fact." Expert testimony is admissible on any subject "sufficiently beyond common experience that the opinion of an expert would assist the trier of fact."

When the trial testimony of an alleged victim of domestic violence is inconsistent with what the victim had earlier told the police, the jurors may well assume that the victim is an untruthful or unreliable witness. And when the victim's trial testimony supports the defendant or minimizes the violence of his actions, the jurors may assume that if there really had been abusive behavior, the victim would not be testifying in the defendant's favor. These are common notions about domestic violence victims.

At trial, expert witness Jeri Parker described the tendency of domestic violence victims to recant previous allegations of abuse as part of the particular behavior patterns commonly observed in abusive relationships. Most abusive relationships begin with a struggle for power and control between the abuser and the victim that later escalates to physical abuse. The initial "tension-building stage" of the "cycle of violence" can appear in deceptively mundane ways, such as complaints about the cleanliness of the house. Often the abuser uses psychological, emotional, or verbal abuse to control the victim. When the victim tries to leave or to assert control over the situation, the abuser may turn to violence as an attempt to maintain control. Later, even if there has been no other episode of violence, the victim may change her mind about prosecuting the abuser and may recant her previous statements.

Here, there was an adequate foundation for that expert testimony, because evidence presented at trial suggested the possibility that Defendant and Kimberly Laforge were in a "cycle of violence" of the type described by expert Jeri Parker. Laforge told Deputy Wheeler that Defendant had complained about the cleanliness of the apartment on the evening of the assault. There was also evidence that Laforge and Defendant also argued that evening about Defendant's failure to take her side in an argument with his cousin (their landlord) regarding the rent, that Defendant told Laforge that if she did not pay the rent she would have to move out, and that he later threatened to kill her if she did leave. Finally, there was evidence that when Laforge actually tried to leave the apartment, Defendant assaulted her. To assist the jury in evaluating this evidence, the trial court properly admitted the expert testimony by Parker.

Defendant asserts that the argument for admitting expert testimony after a single incident of violence is circular, because the jury must first find the preliminary fact of abuse to be true before it may consider the expert evidence. We do not share that view. The argument that evidence relating to credibility cannot be admitted until the underlying charge has been found true was rejected in other domestic violence cases. To be sure, this kind of evidence cannot be admitted to prove the occurrence of the charged crimes. There must be independent evidence of domestic violence -- otherwise the expert testimony about how victims of domestic violence behave would lack foundation. Here, such evidence was supplied by both Laforge's trial testimony in court and by her earlier statement to Deputy Wheeler.

Once there is evidence from which the trier of fact could find the charges true, evidence relating to the credibility of the witnesses becomes relevant and admissible. There is no rule requiring a preliminary finding that the charged act of abuse occurred before the jury can consider the evidence relating to credibility.

We therefore conclude that the trial court did not err in admitting expert testimony concerning the behavior of victims of domestic violence even though the evidence showed only one violent incident.

Affirmed.

People v. Slater

Columbia Court of Appeal (2008)

A jury convicted defendant, John Slater, of three serious felonies based on an incident in which he broke his wife's leg. He was convicted of inflicting corporal injury on a spouse, and assault with force likely to cause great bodily injury both with enhancements for personally inflicting great bodily injury in circumstances involving domestic violence. Defendant was sentenced to nine years and eight months in prison.

On appeal he contends it was error to admit evidence of battered woman's syndrome.

FACTS

In the early morning of May 13, 2001, Officer Brandon Bean was dispatched to the Roseville Medical Center emergency room on a report of spousal abuse. There he found Sonia Slater (Sonia). She smelled slightly of alcohol and was in pain. Her right bicep and her right ankle were bruised.

Sonia had a fractured dislocation of the fibula just below the knee and the strong ligament was torn apart. The injury required surgery in which a screw was inserted. Sonia had six weeks of painful rehabilitation and still had some pain at the time of trial.

In May 2001, Sonia had been married to Defendant for three years. They had two children together and she had a daughter from a previous relationship. Their marriage had a lot of friction and was often violent. At trial, Sonia testified to four acts of domestic violence by Defendant. In January 1999, Sonia's daughter wanted to watch television and Defendant objected. He called the girl names. Sonia stood up for her daughter and Defendant got angry. He choked Sonia and hit her with his fists, calling her a fat, worthless whore. Sonia called the police and Defendant left. Defendant was convicted of misdemeanor spousal abuse.

Sonia got back together with Defendant because she was pregnant with their second child. Defendant worked and Sonia stayed home with the children. In May 2000, Sonia was watching television with a friend. Defendant did not like the show they were watching. He grabbed Sonia and she thought he was going to kiss her. Instead, he bit through her lip, leaving a scar. Sonia did not report the incident because she was afraid of Defendant.

On May 4, 2001, Sonia went to a friend's house after dinner. Defendant told her to be home at 8:00 or 9:00 p.m. She got home between 10:00 and 11:00 p.m. and went to bed. At 1:00 a.m. she awoke with Defendant on top of her, choking her. Sonia woke her daughter, who called 911. When the police arrived, Sonia told them not to arrest Defendant because she did not want to be on welfare.

The police officer who responded to the call testified that Sonia was under the influence of alcohol. The closet doors were smashed. When he tried to take a statement, Sonia was distracted and got up to wash dishes or check on the children, who were confused. Sonia told the officer she was fed up and wanted Defendant out of there because he was "screwing around" on her. Defendant returned and told the officer that Sonia started the fight when she came home, accusing Defendant of cheating on her. In frustration, Defendant pounded the closet doors. He went to the couch and Sonia followed and hit him. He then followed her to the bedroom where he may have choked her. There was no trauma visible on Sonia's neck; she had a bruise on her arm. Defendant had bruises, scratches and a bite mark. The officer determined Defendant was the primary aggressor, but referred the case for further investigation because there might be cause to arrest Sonia.

After the May 4th incident, Sonia decided she had had enough abuse and left Defendant. Defendant wanted to reconcile and called her constantly. On May 12th, Sonia went to a barbecue in Roseville, where she had three or four beers. Afterwards she went to the Onyx Bar.

Later Defendant came in the bar and asked her, "Are you with this jerk now?" She told him, "Screw you!" and left the bar and walked towards her car. Defendant grabbed her by the arm and told her he was taking her home. He took her keys and tried to get her to drink some tequila. He threw her to the ground and kicked her. Three men came to Sonia's rescue. They got her keys and chased Defendant off.

Sonia drove to a friend's house. She called another friend, who took her to the hospital. The hospital staff called the police.

After she was released from the hospital, Sonia heard from her mother and Defendant that if she did not drop the charges, Defendant would do things to her. She obtained a restraining order. Defendant still called her. Sometimes he said he loved her and wanted to get back together. Other times he told her she was a worthless whore who would get AIDS. He offered her money for the kids and wanted her to drop the restraining order.

On June 22nd, Sonia reported her car window was broken. She told the officer that Defendant called and said his sister broke it. He told Sonia he would fix her window if she dropped the divorce and the restraining order. He also offered to help with her bills.

On cross-examination, defense counsel attacked Sonia's credibility. Sonia did not tell Officer Bean that Defendant kicked her; she told him Defendant had grabbed her arm and pushed her down. Counsel questioned why Sonia's story was getting worse; now she claimed Defendant stomped on her leg. Sonia's version of the May 4th incident also did not match the officer's version. Sonia said she may have "sugar-coated" reports to the police.

The defense succeeded in portraying Sonia in a negative light. Sonia denied having an affair while married and later admitted it. She admitted she drank and used drugs, including using methamphetamine. Sonia denied making a throat-slashing motion while a witness was testifying in another case. A court reporter saw it.

In an interview with the police, Defendant admitted going to the Onyx Bar and talking to Sonia. He claimed Sonia was drunk and she stumbled and fell. He denied he pushed her.

Over defense objection, Linda Barnard (Dr. Barnard), a licensed marriage/family therapist, testified at length on domestic violence and the battered woman's syndrome. Dr. Barnard testified that domestic violence is the physical, emotional, sexual or verbal abuse between two persons in an intimate relationship. She explained various myths and misconceptions about domestic violence and battered women. Many believe the woman is masochistic and enjoys the abuse, which is not true. Women stay in abusive relationships for many reasons, including emotional dependency, financial dependency, concern for their children, religious beliefs and family pressure. The primary reasons for staying are love and fear. Many believe the violence stops if a woman leaves, but that is not true, as 75 percent are abused after they leave. It is a myth that domestic violence is limited. It is very underreported, with only 10 to 25 percent of victims reporting, and 95 percent of victims are women. Only 2 percent of reports are false. According to studies, domestic violence affects 1.4 million women per year. One-third to one-half of women will be physically assaulted at some time by an intimate partner.

Mutual combat is a myth; when women hit, it is usually in self-defense and women are normally more seriously injured. It is a myth that women are quick to call the police. In fact, they avoid reporting abuse for the same reasons they stay in abusive relationships. Also, they may be embarrassed. It is a misconception that battered women are passive. Some are, but most fight back at some point and some fight back all the time. The battered woman may precipitate violence in order to have some control.

The cycle of violence has three stages: tension building, an acute episode, and a honeymoon or tranquility stage. In one-third of the cases, there is no honeymoon stage, only tension and aggression.

The characteristics of a battered woman are anxiety, depression, minimizing, denial, sleep disturbances, fear, symptoms similar to post-traumatic stress disorder, hypervigilance and a high startle response. Battered women frequently self-medicate with drugs or alcohol. Dr. Barnard described battered women as exhibiting a "flat affect," that is, they show no emotion. It may be triggered by disassociation in traumatic situations. They also exhibit piecemeal memory, that is, remembering events only pieces at a time.

The prosecution gave Dr. Barnard a hypothetical situation: There is a three-year relationship with numerous incidents of domestic violence, some reported and some not, culminating in a broken leg. During rehabilitation, the victim gets a restraining order and then receives calls that the batterer is wasting money on drugs. The victim then calls him, using foul language, and comments that he is not supplying diapers and food and that he is using the drug, ecstasy. Would that be surprising behavior from a battered woman? Dr. Barnard said, no. If the battered woman is safe, she may initiate serious anger toward the batterer.

DISCUSSION

The People sought to admit evidence of battered woman's syndrome (BWS). The defense demanded that the prosecution identify the specific myth or misconception such evidence would address. The court held a hearing under Evidence Code section 402 to consider the relevance of the evidence. The prosecutor identified three areas of BWS the expert would address: why women stay, the myth that victims are always meek and mild, and the cycle of violence.

Dr. Barnard testified at length at the hearing. The defense identified ten points she had raised and argued all of them were irrelevant and not supported by evidence. The ten points were: (1) why women stay; (2) the myth that victims are always meek and mild; (3) the cycle of violence; (4) what happens when women leave; (5) control issues; (6) post-traumatic stress disorder; (7) the effect of drugs and alcohol; (8) the myth of mutual combat; (9) a profile of batterers; and, (10) a hypothetical. The trial court ruled all the BWS testimony was admissible, except as relating to post-traumatic stress disorder and profiling.

There are two major components of a relevance analysis in admitting BWS testimony. First, there must be sufficient evidence to support the contention that BWS applies to the woman involved. Here, there was evidence to support a finding that Sonia was a battered woman. She testified her marriage to Defendant was characterized by friction and violence. And she testified about four specific incidents of domestic violence.

Second, in order for BWS testimony to be admissible, there must be a contested issue as to which it is probative. BWS testimony is admissible to disabuse the jury of widely held misconceptions or popular myths. It is often admitted to address recantation and reunion by the battered woman, especially where such actions are used to attack the victim's credibility.

Defendant contends the trial court erred in "blithely" finding that the wholesale introduction of BWS expert testimony is warranted in every case. This contention misreads the record. Rather than simply admit all BWS testimony, the court held a hearing and ruled which portions were admissible, excluding proffered testimony on post-traumatic stress disorder and profiling of batterers. It is not an abuse of discretion to permit some leeway in prosecution questioning of a BWS expert. When BWS testimony is properly admitted, testimony about the hypothetical abuser and hypothetical victim is needed for BWS to be understood. To the extent that the expert testimony suggests hypothetical abuse that is worse than the case at trial, it may even work to the defendant's advantage. In any event, limiting the testimony to the victim's state of mind without some explanation of the types of behaviors that trigger BWS could easily defeat the purpose for which the expert is called, which is to explain the victim's actions in light of the abusive conduct.

Defendant contends testimony about the myth that battered women are passive was irrelevant because the evidence showed that Sonia was not passive. Defendant misunderstands the point of the expert's testimony. Dr. Barnard testified that most battered women fight back some of the time and some do all of the time. The evidence that Sonia fought back on occasion fit into this described syndrome.

Defendant contends evidence about the cycle of violence was irrelevant as there was no evidence about such a cycle in this case. This evidence provides the type of explanation that is necessary for BWS to be understood.

Defendant objects to the testimony about mutual combat. Dr. Barnard's testimony in the Section 402 hearing on this subject was confusing as she seemed to suggest there was almost never mutual combat because men are stronger. She testified men are the primary aggressors 95 percent of the time. At trial she testified a battered woman usually engages in serious violence, other than pushing and shoving, only to defend herself, and research has shown men are the predominant aggressors. Thus, the actual BWS testimony was less objectionable than that proffered. Moreover, any error in admitting this testimony was harmless because there was no evidence to suggest the broken leg incident was the result of mutual combat.

Defendant contends it was error to permit Dr. Barnard to testify that drug and alcohol abuse escalates domestic violence and that a batterer may encourage the victim to use drugs and alcohol. Defendant contends there was no evidence that Defendant caused Sonia to use drugs and alcohol. There was evidence that Sonia had used drugs with Defendant, but there was ample evidence that she drank heavily in his absence. The most pertinent portion of Dr. Barnard's testimony on this point was that battered women often self-medicate with drugs or alcohol.

Finally, Defendant contends the BWS testimony served as a testimonial to Sonia's credibility. Although the trial court excluded any testimony about post-traumatic stress disorder, Dr. Barnard used the terms "flat affect" and "piecemeal memory" to explain why Sonia did not tell anyone at the hospital about Defendant "stomping" or "kicking" her leg.

We find no error in the admission of the BWS testimony. There was evidence Sonia was a battered woman and the testimony was relevant to explain some of her behavior, such as her failure to leave Defendant sooner and to minimize some early violence.

The judgment is affirmed.

SELECTED ANSWER 1

MEMORANDUM

TO: Deputy District Attorney Milo Ward
FROM: Applicant
DATE: August 1, 2013
RE: People v. Draper

Admissibility of the Testimony of the Expert Witness Professor Simoni

The people in the current case of People v. Draper intend to call a domestic violence expert, Professor Pamela Simoni, to explain that it is typical in battering situations for women to recant. Professor Simoni plans to do this by discussing battered women's syndrome (BWS). Per the defense's request, there was an evidentiary hearing under Evidence Code Section 402 to determine the admissibility of Professor Simoni's testimony. It is important to note that Professor Simoni was qualified as an expert under Evidence Code Section 801.

Professor Simoni's testimony will only be admissible if it is found to be (1) relevant and (2) if the court does not exclude the evidence based on the fact that its probative value is substantially outweighed by the danger of undue prejudice.

Relevance

According to People v. Slater, there are two major components of a relevance analysis in admitting BWS testimony. First, there must be sufficient evidence to support the contention that BWS applies to the woman involved. Second, in order for BWS testimony to be admissible, there must be a contested issue as to which it is probative.

(a) Sufficiency of Evidence Supporting the Contention that BWS Applies to Victim Sarah Morris

In order for BWS testimony to be found relevant, there must be sufficient evidence to support the contention that BWS applies to the woman involved. In other words, there must be sufficient factual evidence to form a foundation that the victim is a nattered woman. Gould. The factual evidence that the victim is a battered woman does not need to be based on proven evidence of abuse. Bowen. Rather, any evidence of prior battery is admissible, and then BWS can be used to assess the credibility of the victim and related evidence of abuse. Bowen.

In People v. Slater, the alleged victim testified to four acts of domestic violence by the defendant. According to the court, that was sufficient factual evidence to form a foundation that the victim was a battered woman, as she testified that her marriage to the defendant was characterized by friction and violence and testified about four specific incidents of domestic violence.

In Gould, however, the court held that expert testimony regarding battered woman's syndrome was inadmissible as irrelevant, because no evidence showed the victim in the case was suffering from battered women's syndrome. The court in Gould based this holding on the fact that this was the first time a battery had been reported, and as such, there was no evidence of a previous battering.

However, in People v. Bowen, the court came to the opposite conclusion. In that case, the concern was that admission of BWS testimony, which goes to the credibility of the victim and helps to explain her story, has the potential to be highly prejudicial to the defendant. Therefore, the defendant argued that evidence of prior battery must be proven before it can be used as a foundation for the admission of BWS testimony. However, the court reasoned that once there is evidence from which the trier of fact can find the charges true, then evidence relating to the credibility of the witnesses becomes relevant and admissible. There is no rule requiring a preliminary finding that the charged act of abuse occurred before the jury can consider the evidence relating to credibility. Therefore, the court held the lower court did not err in admitting expert testimony concerning the behavior of victims of domestic violence even though the evidence showed only one violent incident.

In Bowen, the court found there was an adequate foundation for expert testimony regarding battered woman's syndrome, because evidence presented at trial suggested the possibility that defendant and the alleged victim were in a "cycle of violence" of the type described by the expert. The court based this on the fact that the alleged victim had told the deputy that the defendant had complained about the cleanliness of the apartment on the evening of the assault. There was also evidence that the alleged victim and the defendant argued that evening about the defendant's failure to take her side in an argument with his cousin (their landlord) regarding the rent, that the defendant had told the alleged victim that if she did not pay the rent she would have to move out, and that the defendant later threatened to kill the alleged victim if she did in fact leave. Finally, the court based this on evidence that when the alleged victim actually tried to leave the apartment, the defendant assaulted her. Ultimately, the court felt the expert testimony was relevant because of this evidentiary foundation of a "cycle of violence" and admitted the expert testimony to assist the jury in evaluating the evidence.

The court further explained that it is not necessary that the jury first find the preliminary fact of abuse to be true before it may consider the expert evidence, as the argument that evidence relating to credibility cannot be admitted until the underlying charge has been found true has been rejected in other domestic violence cases. While the court did acknowledge that evidence of this kind cannot be admitted to prove the occurrence of the charged crimes, it also stated that that there must be independent evidence of domestic violence to give foundation for the admission of the expert testimony.

Here, the court held that evidence is to be supplied by both the alleged victim's trial testimony in court and by her earlier statement to the deputy. The court explained that the evidence would assist the trier of fact in evaluating the credibility of the victim's trial testimony and earlier statements to the police, by providing relevant information about the tendency of victims of domestic violence later to recant or minimize their description of that violence.

In the current case, like in Slater, there is evidence that the victim and defendant's marriage is characterized by friction. In the 402 hearing, the victim's brother testified that the defendant recently lost his job and was a lot moodier and got upset a lot more. He explained that he wanted the victim to quit her job and that he was making the victim give him all of her paychecks because he couldn't trust her anymore. The victim's brother also testified to the fact that the victim was recently feeling horrible, anxious and depressed and, because of the defendant's behavior, that she couldn't do anything right. This is also similar to the constant complaining about cleanliness of the house which was found to be sufficient in Bowen. In Bowen, the court also considered the testimonial evidence from the event at issue, holding that it went to evidence of a "cycle of violence." Here, there is the evidence from the 911 call, as well as the victim's brother's testimony about the night in question. There is also the testimonial evidence from the victim's dentist, Dr. Tucker, who testified that the victim's injury was from a high-impact blow, not a low-impact blow.

On the whole, given the testimony as to the night in question, as well as evidence of a marriage characterized by friction, there is likely sufficient evidence supporting the contention that the victim, Sarah Morris, is a battered woman. As such, the evidence is likely sufficient to show that BWS does in fact apply to her.

(b)   Existence of a Contested Issue as to Which the BWS Testimony is Probative

Under People v. Slater, in order for BWS testimony to be admissible, there must be a contested issue as to which it is probative. The court in Slater did not feel it is appropriate to admit all BWS testimony, but rather to hold a 402 hearing to rule on which portions are admissible, as here. However, the court did not feel it is an abuse of discretion to permit some leeway in prosecution questioning of a BWS expert. In fact, the court explained BWS testimony is admissible to disabuse the jury of widely held misconceptions or popular myths. It is often admitted to address recantation and reunion by the battered woman, especially where such actions are used to attack the victim's credibility. In <u>Slater</u>, the court found the BWS testimony evidence was relevant to explain some of the victim's behavior, such as her failure to leave the defendant sooner and to minimize some early violence. However, it did make sure to exclude BWS testimony relating to post-traumatic stress disorder and profiling.

In the current case, expert Professor Simoni's testimony regarding BWS covered eight different topics: (1) The Typical Profile of a Batterer; (2) Patterns of behavior of batterers and battering victims; (3) The cycle of violence; (4) Recantation; (5) Behavior right after the abuse; (6) The So-Called "Window" and Why it closes; (7) Why victims return to the relationship; and (8) The posing of a hypothetical. Each will be admissible only if it is probative as to a contested issue, as long as it is not later excluded under CEC 252 for undue prejudice.

(1) *The Typical Profile of a Batterer*

In <u>Slater</u>, the court excluded this testimony as an inadmissible portion of the expert's testimony regarding BWS. Here, Professor Simoni explained in her testimony there was no typical profile in terms of socioeconomic status or race of a male batterer, as all classes and races are represented. While this testimony actually explains that there is no typical profile, it will still likely be inadmissible as not probative of a contested issue, as was done in Slater. Profiling has a high potential for creating undue influence on the jury and is not an issue in this case.

(2) *Patterns of behavior of batterers and battering victims*

Here, Professor Simoni went into great depth explaining the patterns of behavior seen in both batterers and battering victims. While the patterns of behavior seen in batterers may be considered to fall into the category of profiling and thus be excluded, that is unlikely. Rather, the court will likely follow the reasoning used in <u>Slater</u> as to character traits and patterns of behavior. The court reasoned that, even where a victim does not possess a particular trait of BWS, or only possesses that trait to a small extent, it is relevant to help the jury ultimately determine whether the victim does in fact suffer from BWS. Following that reasoning, the court admitted evidence that battered women are passive, despite the defendant's argument this was irrelevant, as the alleged victim did not possess that trait. This is because there was evidence that the alleged victim exhibited this behavior sometimes and therefore fit into the described syndrome.

Here, evidence as to battering victim's patterns of behavior, under that reasoning, is definitely relevant to determine whether Sarah Morris fits into the described syndrome. Furthermore, the court is likely to find that evidence as to batterer patterns of behavior is admissible to also aid in determining whether the victim fits into a described syndrome. This is because the victim's behavior may be a response to typical batterer behavior and help to explain or illuminate typical battering victim behavior in Sarah Morris. Ultimately, then, the jury will better be able to determine whether BWS applies in the current case.

(3)   *The cycle of violence*

Here, Professor Simoni described in her BWS testimony the "cycle of violence" that typically occurs once a woman has committed to a relationship with a batterer. In Slater, the court held this evidence describing the cycle of violence provides the type of explanation that is necessary for BWS to be understood. Here, Professor gave a very similar explanation to the one used in Slater. As such, this evidence is likely admissible as probative of a contested issue in the case.

(4)   *Recantation*

In her testimony regarding BWS, Professor Simoni explained the phenomenon of "recanting," wherein about 80 percent of the time, a woman who has been initially assaulted will recant, change or minimize her story. She further explained that this does not happen only after there has been a continuing pattern of abuse and is actually more likely to occur after the first imncident. This information is highly probative of a contested issue, as Sarah Morris has in fact recanted on her story. As such, the testimony is likely admissible.

(5) *Behavior right after the abuse*

Here, Professor Simoni described in her testimony the typical behavior of the victim of the abuse right after the abuse occurs, which usually involves terror and shock. In Slater, while the court did not allow evidence of PTSD, it did allow use of the terms "flat affect" and "piecemeal memory" to explain why the victim did not tell anyone at the hospital about the defendant injuring her. As such, here, as long as Professor Simoni does not go as far as to include testimony regarding PTSD, but rather limits hre testimony to an explanation of the victim's behavior as a possible side effect of BWS, the testimony is likely admissible

(6) *The So-Called "Window" and Why it closes*

After describing typical victim behavior right after the abuse, Professor Simoni explained the idea of the "window." Specifically, when the actual violent event occurs, the victim is able to feel and recall the details of the event for a short period. That short window tends to stay open only if the woman leaves the relationship and has support in the outside community. However, Professor Simoni went on to explain that the window will in fact close when the woman has contact with the batterer. She also gave many reasons for the closing, such as kind treatment from the batterer, threats if she talks about the event, and even financial fears. If a victim wishes for the relationship to continue, she will change the story to sound less harsh and even lie about the event. Because of this phenomenon, women are most likely to be honest within the first 24-48 hours after the incident.

This information is highly probative of a contested issue here. This is because Sarah Morris did in fact change her story after the "window" closed – claiming later that the violence was accidental – and she returned to her husband. As such, the testimony is likely admissible.

(7) *Why victims return to the relationship*

Here, Professor Simoni explained that women do tend to return to their abusers and why. Again, here, because, Sarah Morris did in fact return to the relationship, this testimony is highly probative as to a contested issue and is likely admissible.

(8) *The posing of a hypothetical*

Professor Simoni also responded to a hypothetical from the judge. According to Slater, when BWS testimony is properly admitted, testimony about the hypothetical abuser and hypothetical vivctim is needed for BWS to be understood. To the extent that the expert testimony suggests hypothetical abuse that is worse than the case at trial, it may even work to the defendant's advantage. In any event, limiting testimony to the victim's state of mind without some explanation of the types of behaviors that trigger BWS could easily defeat the purpose for which the expert is called, which is to explain the victim's actions in light of the abusive conduct. Here, then, the posing of the hypothetical to expert Professor Simoni was equally needed for BWS to be understood and as such, admissible.

CEC 352 Exclusion for Undue Prejudice

Under Evidence Code Section 352, the court in its discretion may exclude evidence if its probative value is substantially outweighed by the probability that its admission will (a) necessitate undue consumption of time or (b) create substantial danger of undue prejudice, of confusing the issues, or of misleading the jury.

In People v. Gould, the court excluded all BWS testimony, finding it to be both irrelevant under the first prong and also posing the danger of undue influence. The court found the testimony to be powerful, authoritative and likely to have an effect on the jury. The expert was presented as a highly qualified expert and gave a lengthy and dramatic testimony. She also explained in detail the several cycles of a typical battering relationship. She extensively described the male batterer, explaining how he first charms, then demeans and insults his partner. She described that he is someone who both psychologically and physically brutalizes a woman to satisfy his need for power and control. Finally, she compared the relationship between a battering man and a battered woman to "Stockholm Syndrome," a condition which occurs when a hostage begins to view her "attacker" as a "good guy." She even went so far as to state that a batterer is often referred to as a "Dr. Jekyll and Mr. Hyde." Given the inflammatory nature of the expert's testimony, the court found the testimony to be highly prejudicial, ultimately concluding that the jury was reasonably likely to reach a result more favorable to the alleged battered had the court originally excluded the expert's testimony regarding battered woman's syndrome.

Here, there are the same concerns. Professor Simoni's testimony certainly poses a high risk of the danger of undue influence on the jury outweighing the probative value. She extensively described typical behavior patterns in the batterer and the victim. That being said, the testimony in Gould, first of all, was found to have very little probative value in that case. Here, as explained above, the portions of Professor Simoni's testimony deemed to be admissible under the relevance test are highly probative of a contested issue. Furthermore, Professor Simoni did not dramatize BWS in the way that was done by the expert in Gould and which worried the court in that case. She made no inflammatory comparisons, and certainly wasn't overly dramatic, which would pose a danger of unduly influencing the jury. Rather, she took care to speak matter-of-factly and present the syndrome in a way that goes to the contested issues, without doing so at the expense of inflaming the jury.

Additionally, the court may work to prevent the risk of undue influence by giving jury instructions limiting the use of the testimony, as was done in People v. Bowen.

Conclusion

Ultimately, it is likely that Professor Simoni's testimony will be found both relevant, except as to the profiling testimony, and not risking the danger of undue influence outweighing probative value. As such, the evidence is likely to be admissible.

SELECTED ANSWER 2

TO: Deputy District Attorney Milo Ward
FROM: Applicant
DATE: August 1, 2013
RE: People v. Draper draft memorandum (internal memo)

You have asked me to draft a memo in which I analyze which portions of Professor Simoni's testimony are admissible, and which portions are not. You have informed me that you will use this internal memo to help you draft the post-hearing brief requested by the judge. I have attached the draft of the memo you requested. Please let me know if you have any questions.

I.   Relevance of the Battered Woman's Syndrome Testimony

Evidence Code Section 801 permits the introduction of testimony by a qualified expert when that testimony may "assist the trier of fact." Expert testimony is admissible on any subject "sufficiently beyond common experience that the opinion of an expert would assist the trier of fact." Section 801. (The defendant has not contested our expert's qualifications, according to the transcript of the hearing.)

There are two major components of a relevance analysis in admitting battered woman's syndrome (BWS) expert testimony. First, "there must be sufficient evidence to support the contention that BWS applies to the woman involved." Second, "there must be a contested issue as to which [BWS testimony] is probative." People v. Slater.

The defendant objects to the subject matter of the expert's testimony because "there is no evidence that Mr. Draper fits the male batterer profile or that Ms. Morris suffers from battered woman's syndrome."

A.   Sufficient Evidence to Support That BWS Applies To Sarah Morris in This Case

Whether expert testimony regarding battered woman's syndrome is admissible in a particular case initially depends on whether that evidence is relevant. Therefore, in making a determination of relevancy, the evidence must support in this particular case "a contention that the petitioner suffered ongoing abuse or battering." People v. Gould. The Gould court held that expert testimony on BWS is relevant if there is a sufficient "factual basis for the fact that petitioner experienced ongoing abuse or battering." Gould. When the existence of a preliminary fact, such as this one regarding ongoing abuse or battering, is disputed, "its existence or nonexistence" must be determined. Columbia Evidence Code Section 402.

Furthermore, the Bowen court stated that "the argument that evidence relating to credibility cannot be admitted until the underlying charge has been found true was rejected in other domestic violence cases." This kind of expert testimony cannot be admitted to prove the occurrence of the charged crimes; there "must be independent evidence of domestic violence—otherwise the expert testimony about how victims of domestic violence behave would lack foundation." Bowen

In the Bowen case, the court found that there was "an adequate foundation" for the BWS expert testimony because evidence presented at trial "suggested the possibility that Defendant and [victim] were in a 'cycle of violence' of the type described" by the expert. The victim had told a police officer that the defendant had complained about the cleanliness of the apartment on the evening of the assault. There was also evidence in the Bowen case that the victim and the defendant had also argued that evening about defendant's failures to support the victim. In the same argument, the defendant had also told the victim that she had to pay rent or move out and then the defendant later threatened to kill the victim. Lastly, there was evidence in the Bowen case to show that when the victim had tried to leave, the defendant assaulted her. All of this evidence is drawn from various, different incidents and occurrences from the same evening. Bowen.

This instant case is comparable to Bowen and shares several similarities in the amount of evidence suggesting a "cycle of violence." See Bowen. On the 911 tape, from June

5, 2012, which was played during the hearing, we see evidence that Horace Draper (Draper) hit Sarah Morris (Morris) in the mouth, causing her to bleed and not be able to breathe. Just like the victim in Bowen told the police officer about defendant's complaining about the cleanliness of the apartment, Sarah had told the 911 dispatcher about her husband's hitting her. The 911 tape also shows Sarah telling the dispatcher that her husband not only hit her but then took away the car keys and took the car. Later testimony from Morris's brother also shows evidence of Morris having a "bloody mouth and a large bruise on her neck and shoulder area."

The testimony of Morris's dentist, Cathy Tucker, also corroborates the brother's testimony: "Ms. Morris came into my office on June 5, 2012 at around 10 a.m. She had a pretty badly split lip, a significantly swollen mouth, extensive bleeding, and a loose tooth . . . The treatment took four and one-half hours." The dentist also testified that the injuries were likely caused by a high-impact blow.

In addition, just as the Bowen court found that the victim and defendant's arguing showed evidence of a "cycle of violence," the court in this case will likely find that Draper and Morris's arguing is evidence of a cycle of violence. According to the testimony of Paul Morris, Draper and his wife, Sarah Morris, had been arguing on that same June 5, 2012 morning, before the assault and incident. Draper and his wife had been arguing because Draper had taken $120 from her purse to pay the gardener.

There is also evidence tending to show an intent by Draper to control Morris based on Paul Morris's testimony. The brother testified that ever since Draper lost his job and Sarah Morris got promoted, Draper was a lot moodier and got upset a lot more and demanded that Sarah Morris quit her job. Draper had told Paul Morris, Sarah's brother, that he was making her give him all her paychecks because he couldn't trust her any more. Sarah Morris had also told her brother about a month before the June 5, 2012 incident that she was feeling "horrible, anxious and depressed." Sarah Morris said she felt like "she couldn't do anything right."

This case is even stronger than the one in Bowen because the evidence and testimony suggests a longer cycle and pattern of abuse and jealousy seems to have spanned more than a month at least, and Morris and Draper have been in a cycle of argument, jealousy, and control since Draper had been fired and Morris got promoted. Whereas the Bowen court analyzed the cycle and events within one evening, the evidence shows a cycle of at least a month. See Bowen. This case is also similar to Slater, where the court also found sufficient evidence to establish a foundation for a cycle of violence.

The evidence in this case would tend to form the basis for a cycle of violence, which our expert will testify as when "the batterer has an absolute need for power and control over his female partner," where the relationship usually follows a three-phase cycle of "tension-building," "actual physical violence," and a "honeymoon" phase.

.

Therefore, there is likely to be a sufficient "factual basis for the fact that petitioner experienced ongoing abuse or battering." Gould. Just as in Bowen, there is an "adequate foundation" for the BWS expert testimony because evidence can be presented to "suggest the possibility that" Draper and Morris were in a cycle of violence of the type described by our expert.

Furthermore, this case is different and distinguishable from Gould because the court in that case found that there was "no evidence, with the exception of the present incident, to indicate [victim] is in a battering relationship." Gould. "A single violent incident, without evidence of other psychological abuse, is not sufficient to establish that a woman suffers from battered woman's syndrome." Gould. Even though Gould and Bowen may seem irreconcilable, Bowen conforms with the Gould court's holding because the incidents in Gould were multiple in the same evening—thus, showing a "cycle." Here, there is evidence to suggest such a cycle because Morris's brother, Paul, has testified that ever since Draper lost his job and Morris got promoted, Draper was a lot moodier and got upset a lot more and told Morris to quit her job and even withheld her paychecks from her because "he couldn't trust her." In addition, Morris had also displayed signs of abuse when she said she felt horrible, anxious and depressed. Such incidents and behavior patterns over at least a month's span are different than just one incident in one night, such as the one in Gould.

B. Contested Issue as to Which BWS Testimony Is Probative

In order for BWS testimony to be admissible, there must be a contested issue as to which it is probative. BWS testimony is admissible to disabuse the jury of widely held misconceptions or popular myths. It is often admitted to address "recantation and reunion by the battered woman, especially where such actions are used to attack the victim's credibility." Slater.

The Slate court found that the BWS testimony was also admissible because there was a contested issue as to which testimony was probative. In Slater, the BWS testimony was admissible to disabuse the jury of widely held misconceptions or popular beliefs, such as "recantation and reunion" by the battered woman.

The instant case is likely similar because a jury or common observers may not find Sarah Morris's previous telephone call to the dispatcher or her conversations with her brother on June 5, 2012, to be credible because she has changed her story. As you have told me, Morris has since changed her story and now states that her injuries were accidental. The BWS testimony of our expert would be probative to help disabuse the jury of common myths or misunderstandings regarding recantation or reunion, just like in Slater and Bowen. Such expert testimony could help explain Sarah Morris's subsequent actions, behavior, and testimony. As the Bowen court wrote: "When the trial testimony of an alleged victim of domestic violence is inconsistent with what the victim earlier told the police, the jurors may well assume that the victim is an untruthful or unreliable witness." Bowen.

C. Unfair Prejudice

Section 352 of the Evidence Code states that a court in its discretion may "exclude evidence if its probative value is substantially outweighed by the probability that its admission will. . .create substantial danger of undue prejudice, of confusing the issues, or of misleading the jury."

The expert testimony of Simoni should only be used to bolster the credibility of Morris's past statements, not to serve as evidence "to prove the occurrence of the charged crimes." Bowen. The instant case may require a jury instruction or limiting instruction of some sort like the ones in Bowen and Slater.

II.   Admissible and Inadmissible Portions of Simoni's Testimony

You have asked me to analyze which portions of Professor Simoni's (Simoni) testimony are admissible, and which portions are not. Based on the evidentiary hearing, Simoni will attempt to testify on the eight following subjects: 1) the typical profile of a batterer; 2) patterns of behavior of batterers and battering victims; 3) the cycle of violence; 4) recantation; 5) behavior right after the abuse; 6) the so-called "window" and why it closes; 7) why victims return to the relationship; and 8) the posing of a hypothetical.

Based on the analysis of the case law and evidence code, there is likely evidence to support testimony on all these topics, except for the first topic, the typical profile of a batterer.

A.   The Typical Profile of a Batterer

As stated before, a court in its discretion may "exclude evidence if its probative value is substantially outweighed by the probability that its admission will . . .create substantial danger of undue prejudice, of confusing the issues, or of misleading the jury." Section 352.

The trial court did not admit such in Slater and the court of appeals affirmed the trial court's holding. Slater. It is not clear from the Slater opinion why the trial court did not admit such expert testimony, but the Gould opinion suggests that such testimony is inadmissible because it would be too prejudicial under Section 352. Gould.

In Gould, the court held that "we cannot ignore" the expert's "powerful testimony and its likely effect on the jury." The expert was presented as authoritative. She had extensively described the profile of the prototypical "male batterer," explaining how "he first charms, then demeans and insults his partner." The expert in Gould described a typical battering man as someone who both psychologically and physically "brutalizes a woman to satisfy his need for power and control." The Gould court found this type of testimony to be too prejudicial.

Our expert, Professor Simoni, is going to give similar expert testimony about the batterer's "typical profile." She said during the preliminary hearing that "there are commonly recurring characteristics of batterers," and that the typical batterer will at first be "charming, romantic and intense." The typical male batterer will also make his partner dependent and attack her self-esteem, just like the expert in Gould said the batterer would brutalize the woman to satisfy his need for power and control.

Our expert also has similar credentials to the one in Gould. The Gould expert was the director of a domestic abuse center, just like Simoni worked as a legal director for a program that was part of a larger domestic violence agency in Oakmont in Sanford County. She also served on several boards that promoted an end to domestic violence. Therefore, based on the Slater and Gould cases, Simoni's testimony regarding any profile of a typical batterer will likely not be admissible because it will be too prejudicial under Section 352 and could mislead the jury.

B. Patterns of Bhavior of Batterers and Battering Victims

See above.

Expert testimony is permitted when the expert is qualified and the testimony may assist the trier of fact and when the testimony is on a subject "beyond common experience." Section 801.

In Bowen, the expert was allowed to testify on particular behavior patterns "commonly observed in abusive relationships." The expert testified that the abuser often uses psychological, emotional, or verbal abuse to control the victim. When the victim tries to leave or to assert control over the situation, the abuser may turn to violence as an attempt to maintain control. Later, even if there has been no other episode of violence, the victim may change her mind about prosecuting the abuser and may recant." Bowen. The court found this evidence relevant, on topic, and not too unfairly prejudicial.

Here, our expert will also testify to similar patterns of behavior of batterers and battering victims. She will testify that the man will start to blame the woman for everything that goes on around him. He will also use "coercion, threats, and intimidation to maintain control of his partner." The pattern of behavior may lead to forcing the female to watch pornographic movies and engage in sexual activities that make the female partner feel guilty—"cross her bottom line." He's able to get her to feel ashamed about things that are going on in the relationship, things that she's "uncomfortable with; then he begins to make threats."

Therefore, because the expert testimony in Bowen and here will be sufficiently similar, a vcourt should likely find this portion admissible.

C.   The Cycle of Violence

See above.

The courts in Slater and Bowen admitted similar evidence regarding the cycle of violence. In Slater, the court affirmed the trial court's admission of this evidence. In Bowen, the expert testified that the cycle of violence has an initial "tension building stage," where the male may make small complaints here and there about, for example, the cleanliness of the house.

Our expert will also give a similar testimony regarding the cycle of violence and the "tension building stage." She stated in her hearing that "during the tension building stage, the batterer criticizes his partner." The man will start to emotionally abuse his partner by calling her names and insulting her. The batterer will then isolate the woman from her friends, coworkers, and family. Economic control is a common element.

Therefore, based on the holdings in Slater and Bowen, a court will likely find that the cycle of violence testimony is also admissible.

D. Recantation

See above.

In Bowen, the expert explained why victims of domestic violence may give conflicting statements: "They may be financially dependent on the defendant. They may be pressured or even threatened, by the defendant or other family members. They may still love the defendant and hope that things will get better." The victim may then change her mind about prosecuting the abuser and may recant her previous statements to the police. The woman will also likely minimize the incident. Bowen. About 80-85 percent of victims actually recant at some point.

Just as in Bowen, Simoni will also give similar testimony about recantation. She will say that "this recanting . . . is more likely to occur after a first incident." A woman will tend to minimize and deny the incident. The woman will engage in self-blame and sort of recast the incident, especially if the relationship continues. The victim also begins to feel guilty and responsible.

Thus, because our expert will give similar testimony in a similar case to that of Bowen, the court will likely also admit this testimony regarding recantation.

E. Behavior Right After the Abuse

See above.

The behavior right after the abuse will be admissible because it is probative and will help the jury to understand why Morris made certain recantations or reunions to her husband. A jury may not totally understand why a woman would return to an abusive spouse, but testimony like our expert's can help them understand and demystify common myths.

F. The "Window" for Truthfulness and Why It Closes

See above.

The expert in Bowen testified that there is typically anywhere between 24 and 48 hours where victims will be truthful about what occurred because they're still angry; they're still scared. But "after they have had time to think about it . . . it is not uncommon for them to change their mind and . . . actually recant at some point in the process." Some victims will lie to the police and attempt to minimize the experience.

Our expert will also give similar testimony regarding the window of truthfulness that can close. The window will stay open "however long the woman has support in the outside community" and "only if she leaves the relationship." "The woman never expected this person that she loves . . . to physically hurt her." The window closes because the batterer starts the honeymoon period. The woman may also lose sight of what actually happened.

Therefore, because the expert testimony about the window closing will be based on similar types of information and patterns of behavior, a court will also likely admit this evidence.

G. Why Victims Return to the Relationship

See above.

In Slater, the court allowed the admission of evidence regarding why women stay and return to the relationship. Also see above in Section D. Our expert will also testify that victims typically and often go back to their abusive lover because "they love them; they're not sure how they can survive on their own; pressure from family and friends; or because their children want to be with their father." The expert's testimony regarding why victims return will also be helpful in disabusing common misconceptions and beliefs by the jury because it would help them understand why Morris would want to return. Thus, the court will likely also admit this testimony because of the similarities between the testimony in Bowen and in this case.

H. The Posing of a Hypothetical

In Slater, the expert was allowed to respond to a hypothetical posed by the prosecutor. The hypothetical was very specific to the alleged facts that actually happened in the Slater case. Similar to the Slater case, our expert will likely be able to testify on the hypothetical posed to her that are similar to the facts in our case. The hypothetical can be helpful to the jury because it ties up all the behaviors and common misconceptions regarding a typical victim who is battered.

The court may say that this testimony is too prejudicial though because it could mislead the jury as to believing that the facts and actions of Draper were in conformity with the hypothetical. A limiting instruction may be needed.

III. Conclusion

Therefore, the testimony is generally admissible and relevant and not too prejudicial if a limiting instruction is given. However, the testimony on a typical batterer's profile will likely not be admitted.

www.ingramcontent.com/pod-product-compliance
Lightning Source LLC
Chambersburg PA
CBHW081733220526

45468CB00008B/2080